A COACH APPROACH TO CHRISTIAN GROWTH

For Group or Individual Study

Volume 1

Rachelle Triay, PCC

A Publication of:

An Encouraged Life

Some of the anecdotal illustrations in this book are true to life and are included with the permission of the persons involved. All other illustrations are composites of real situations, and any resemblance to people living or dead is coincidental.

Find Rachelle here:
Website: AnEncouragedLife.com
Email: Info@AnEncouragedLife.com
Facebook: Facebook.com/AnEncouragedLife
Instagram: Instagram.com/AnEncouragedLife
LinkedIn: https://www.linkedin.com/in/rachelle-triay-ael/

ISBN-978-1-7355477-0-1
Library of Congress Control Number: 2020943909

Published by:
An Encouraged Life, LLC, P.O. Box 2703, Mandeville, LA 70470

Printed in the United States of America

We seek **G**od

by **R**eflecting,

through **O**bservable actions,

and **W**ith others.

For Louis.
I choose to GROW with you.

1 Timothy 4:7

Train yourself for godliness. (ESV)

Contents

Acknowledgements

The culmination of this book could not have been achieved without the help of so many. Writing a book took a level of discipline and determination I rarely have had to muster and having friends and family to cheer me on was crucial.

First, I want to thank my editor, Debbie Cannizzaro, who thoroughly and completely believed in this book even in its beginning stages when it was nothing more than a pile of thoughts. She patiently, lovingly, and brilliantly encouraged me to achieve excellence. I am so grateful that God put us together for such a time as this!

My family, who I love with all my heart, also deserves much thanks and praise.

My husband, Louis, has supported my many ideas through the years, but most especially this one. From cooking dinner when I was working late on the book, to understanding when I needed to put extra hours into it, he has been there for me. He listens to my ideas, my struggles, and my dreams, and shares in the successes and disappointments along the way. Thank you, Lou, for standing by my side and helping my dream become a reality.

My daughter, Amanda, donated hours of her time, talents, and resources to create the videos for this book. She has amazing gifts, and she willingly and lovingly volunteered to tackle this substantial component of the book for me. She patiently helped and guided me in so many areas as I often bombarded her with questions and thoughts about marketing, business, and so much more. She and her husband, Christian, have encouraged and supported me along this journey.

My son, Alexander, is a wonderful encourager. He is wise beyond his years and is an excellent listener. When I would get overwhelmed, he would calm me. He would talk me through concepts and ideas, quiet my mind when it was racing, and has been an untiring, tremendous support.

My mom, Janice, has encouraged and supported me through this writing endeavor. She is also a fantastic listener and never tired of hearing about the book's progress. Her unending belief in me always puts wind beneath my wings. Thanks, Mom, for running errands, providing meals, and filling in the gap for our family where needed.

Thank you to my friends who have been there for me through the book writing process. These are my prayer warriors—amazing women who know the power of prayer and consistently interceded on my behalf. They have supported me, listened to me, been there for me, and celebrated with me along the way. I am so grateful God has put each and every one of you in my life.

Much appreciation to those who read drafts and gave me valued constructive feedback. The input was invaluable.

Finally, I want to thank Pastor Danny Mequet and his wife, Missy, as well as Pastor Chris Callahan for reviewing the book with me. I value the blessing of my church on this project.

I am blessed beyond belief to be surrounded by so many people who love me, want the best for me, and want to see me shine! I love you all!

Introduction

Welcome aboard this journey of growth. The GROW curriculum has been created for people who want to GROW in their relationship with God.

As a Life Coach, my passion is partnering with Christ-Followers who want to maximize their potential for Kingdom work. I have had the privilege of partnering with clients from all over the world to encourage growth. I want to partner with you through this book.

GROW is for people who want to live out their Christian life intentionally by learning, setting goals, being challenged, and growing in faith and in relationship with our Creator.

Writing this GROW book is a direct result of stepping out of my comfort zone in obedience to something God placed on my heart. As with most things in my life, it did not happen gracefully, but with the Holy Spirit, it was grace-filled. God continued to gently nudge me in the right direction. I was often overwhelmed, but then I would be overwhelmed with His love. God is faithful. Step by step this project eventually started to take shape. I often ask my clients the question, "How do you eat an elephant?" And of course, the answer is, "One bite at a time."

When the road gets hard, do not quit.

When you are unsure of your next steps, pray and seek counsel, then keep moving.

GROW is for people who want to live out their Christian life intentionally by learning, setting goals, being challenged, and growing in faith and in relationship with our Creator.

If God can use me, He can use you. Lean in, listen, obey. Then step back in awe at what God can do with a willing vessel. God wants you to GROW.

WHAT IS GROW?

GROW is for people who love Jesus. Whether you are a new believer, or have been a Christ-Follower for years, you are welcome here—as long as you are ready to learn and grow.

We have to ***choose*** growth. Rarely does growth happen without us becoming intentional. This table is a motivator because we want our lives to align with these synonyms and definitely not the antonyms:

	SYNONYMS	ANTONYMS
GROWTH	• Advance • Boost • Build-up • Gain • Improvement • Increase • Maturation • Success	• Decrease • Diminishment • Failure • Lessening • Stagnation • Underdevelopment

When talking about my relationship with God, or any other area of my life, I want to choose to GROW. Incidentally, my waistline is contradictory to this. It grows when I ignore it and only decreases when I am intentional!

Farming is a good illustration for GROW.

A farmer has a plot of land that he has prepared. If he plants tomato seeds and tends to them, what will he get? Tomatoes, of course. In the same way, if he plants squash seeds, what will he get? You guessed it. He gets squash. What does he get if he plants nothing? Did you answer nothing? Nope—he gets weeds.

It is important to be intentional about continuing to GROW in our relationship with God. With each goal we write, it is like planting a seed. When we water it, it will grow and produce fruit. If you have ever planted a garden before, you know that gardens take work. If you do not check on it daily and tend to it, you will not get much fruit. When I committed to watering my tomato plants twice a day, and spent time pruning and trellising them, I had to get a ladder to harvest the fruit. The plants had grown nearly eight feet tall and were full of large, juicy tomatoes. The same thing will happen with your relationship with God if you intentionally tend to it.

This book is a tool to encourage growth in your Christian walk. I want to grow good and plentiful fruit! I want to carefully tend to my relationship with God and grow to produce the Kingdom fruit God created me to produce. This is living a purpose-filled life with intentionality, and I hope you will join me. Together we can impact this world in a mighty way.

GROW is an acronym defining a system to promote growth in the Christian walk.

We seek **G**od
by **R**eflecting,
through **O**bservable actions,
and **W**ith others.

First, as Christ-Followers, **we seek God**. We desire to know more about our Creator and GROW in the image of Jesus.

The next component of GROW is to decide which areas currently need growth. This is accomplished **by Reflecting**. We reflect on God's greatness, then reflect on who He made us to be. We reflect on where we are so we can measure if growth has occurred. Finally, we reflect on what the ideal outcomes of our growth will look like.

The ultimate purpose of GROW is to encourage you to grow in your relationship with God.

The next step to intentional growth is to set goals—or **through Observable action** steps. This is where you create your plan for growth. What steps will you take to reach your desired outcome in a particular area of your faith walk?

Finally, we are not created to be alone. Fellowship with like-minded believers will aid in reaching your goals. You will have more success in GROW if you partner **with Others**. Whether aligning with an accountability partner, joining a small group, or partnering with a friend, having people alongside will encourage growth. This will also give you someone to celebrate with when reaching growth milestones, which will also encourage you to continue to GROW!

We are called to GROW, but we are not called to grow in every area all at once.

HOW IS THIS CURRICULUM DIFFERENT?

As a Life Coach, I am passionate about assisting my clients in setting and reaching goals. What I discovered is that while people were quick to make goals in areas such as business, sales, health, and finances, goal setting in the area of faith/spirituality was rarely considered, yet this area is foundational to all others.

The purpose of this book is to encourage you to prayerfully evaluate and set goals in the faith/spirituality areas of your life so that you will GROW in your relationship with God. This book will encourage you to determine your goals and be accountable to take steps toward achieving those goals. The purpose is growth.

The purpose is change. The purpose is to move you into action and mature you as a believer so you will grow in your relationship with God.

SETTING YOURSELF UP FOR SUSTAINABLE GROWTH

As you go through each chapter, I encourage you to pick just one or two of the topics to set immediate goals. Once you have taken steps in those areas, then add another goal. This will keep you from getting overwhelmed with too many goals at the same time.

We are called to GROW, but we are not called to grow in every area all at once. Each person's growth journey will look different depending on their season of life, personal conviction, and worldview. Do not compare yourself to others when setting goals. You are a unique individual with your very own gifts, talents, and abilities. Therefore, where God is calling you to go, what God is calling you to do, and who God is calling you to be will be different from every other person on this planet. Ask the Holy Spirit to guide you and take a baby step. You will find tips on creating goals in the "Goal Setting Success" section of the book.

You are a unique individual with your very own gifts, talents, and abilities. Therefore, where God is calling you to go, what God is calling you to do, and who God is calling you to be will be different from every other person on this planet.

HEART CHECK - THE MOST IMPORTANT PART

Before you set out on this journey, know that God loves you right now, right where you are. We cannot make God love us anymore or any less. It does not matter how much you do or how much you GROW. God's love for you does not change. It is an eternal, unfathomable pure love. This is important and I hope you understand just how much you are loved.

The GROW journey is about the heart; therefore, this curriculum should not be done out of obligation. God desires a relationship with us. We are called to draw near to Him. Each chapter in GROW can help us deepen our relationship with our Creator. Since this is of primary importance, I will remind you about it in each chapter.

GROW is about relationship, not about rules. I have seen clients get so caught up in checklists and action steps that they forget the why behind their actions. People have a tendency to go into autopilot mode and lose focus of purpose. GROW is a tool to assist you in growing closer to God. It is meant to foster growth in your relationship with your Creator. It is not meant to bog you down with more checklists. The why behind GROW is a flourishing relationship with God.

I am excited about this journey we are embarking upon. Commit to GROW in faith, dive deeper, set goals, be intentional, point each other to Jesus, and hold each other accountable in love.

You only have one today, one tomorrow. You only have one life. Let's make the most of it. Let's choose to GROW!

It does not matter how much you do or how much you GROW. God's love for you does not change.

OUR HELPER—THE HOLY SPIRIT

When Jesus ascended to heaven, He told us He would send a Helper, the Holy Spirit.

John 14:26

But the Helper, the Holy Spirit, whom the Father will send in my name, he will teach you all things and bring to your remembrance all that I have said to you. (ESV)

When we accept Jesus as our Lord and Savior, we receive the Holy Spirit:

Acts 2:38

And Peter said to them, "Repent and be baptized every one of you in the name of Jesus Christ for the forgiveness of your sins, and you will receive the gift of the Holy Spirit." (ESV)

As believers, the Holy Spirit lives inside us to guide us, comfort us, and grow us through the process of sanctification. He intercedes on our behalf, teaches us, and gives us gifts so we can do Kingdom work here on earth.

1 Corinthians 6:19-20

Or do you not know that your body is a temple of the Holy Spirit within you, who you have from God? You are not your own, for you were bought with a price. So glorify God in your body. (ESV)

The Holy Spirit is God. As you seek to GROW, I want to encourage you to embrace the gift of the Holy Spirit. As a believer, He is there for you, inside you, ready and willing to guide you on the path He laid out for you. You are made with a purpose that only you can fulfill. The Holy Spirit will help you achieve that purpose.

LET'S JUMP IN!

As a Life Coach, my job is to assist my clients in discerning what is important to them, encourage them to focus on growing in those areas, and hold

The why behind GROW is a flourishing relationship with God.

As you seek to GROW, I want to encourage you to tap into the gift of the Holy Spirit. He is there for you, inside you, ready and willing to guide you on the path that He laid out for you.

When I am living with an eternal, Kingdom perspective, then growing in relationship with my Creator must rise to the top of my priorities.

them accountable. This is what I want to do for you. I hope that each of you will be encouraged. You can do this! I believe in you. I want you to experience a deeper relationship with God because over time, just like the tomatoes in my garden thrived when I focused on them, your relationship with God will also thrive.

The fruit of the Spirit will grow. I want this for you. God wants this for you. I believe it is attainable through GROW.

Galatians 5:22

But the fruit of the Spirit is love, joy, peace, patience, kindness, goodness, faithfulness, gentleness, self-control; against such things there is no law.

There is Kingdom work for every one of us to do. Let's GROW together in our faith, focused on Jesus while encouraging each other to take steps toward maturing as Christ-Followers. Ultimately, we can powerfully impact the world with Christ's love. When I am living with an eternal Kingdom perspective, then growing in relationship with my Creator will rise to the top of my priorities. One day we all hope to hear our Lord and Savior say, "Well done, my good and faithful servant."

Matthew 25:21

His master said to him, 'Well done, good and faithful servant. You have been faithful over a little; I will set you over much. Enter into the joy of your master.'

Be Encouraged,

Rachelle

INTRODUCTION VIDEO

*To enhance your learning experience, scan the QR Code or visit **AnEncouragedLife.com** to watch the supplemental video for this chapter.*

VIDEO LESSONS

You will find video lessons after each chapter. These were created to enhance and supplement your learning while encouraging you to GROW. The videos can be found at AnEncouragedLife.com, or if you have a QR reader on your phone or device, scanning the image above will bring you directly to the video.

Please take a few minutes to watch the introductory video.

NOTES ● THOUGHTS ● INSIGHTS

To set you up for success, please review this section before jumping into the following chapters.

Goal Setting Success

QUOTES ABOUT GOAL SETTING SUCCESS

What you get by achieving your goals is not as important as what you become by achieving your goals.[1]

-Zig Ziglar

The tragedy in life doesn't lie in not reaching your goal. The tragedy lies in having no goal to reach. It isn't a calamity to die with dreams unfulfilled, but it is certainly a calamity not to dream. It is not a disaster to be unable to capture your ideal, but it is a disaster to have no ideal to capture.[2]

-Benjamin E. Mays

Your future is created by what you do today, not tomorrow.[3]

-Robert Kiyosaki

Fundamentals

Goal Setting Success

The purpose of GROW is to encourage you to set goals so you can experience growth in your relationship with God. Before we begin to explore the topics in which we will set goals, my desire is to thoroughly equip you so you can experience success. I want to share with you some important information from my Coaching Tool Box. In this chapter, we will review ten tips for goal setting success and take an in depth look at SMART goals. These tips will set you up to succeed when setting and reaching goals for your faith walk and any area of your life.

10 TIPS FOR GOAL SETTING SUCCESS

Each person is different so goals will vary for every individual. When I work with people to set goals, we develop a vision for the outcome of the goal, discuss the why behind the goal, and spend time thinking about what might get in the way of success. We also brainstorm ideas to overcome potential obstacles. It is important to define the area in which you are currently setting goals so you will be able to effectively look back and measure if growth has occurred.

The list below includes some ideas to improve your success when creating goals.

Success comes when your goals are aligned with God's goals for your life, so always pray before setting goals.

1. Pray and seek guidance from God.

Success comes when your goals are aligned with God's goals for your life, so always pray before setting goals.

Your goals are not what you think your husband or wife wants you to do, or your parent wants you to do, or what you think the world thinks you should do. Goals are between you and God. Earnestly seek the Holy Spirit in your goal setting so you can experience success. This is a logical first step for Christ-Followers since we know God is in control and His will for our lives is most important to us.

Proverbs 16:9

The heart of man plans his way, but the Lord establishes his steps. (ESV)

When I create goals, I want them drenched in godly wisdom.

James 1:5

If any of you lacks wisdom, let him ask God, who gives generously to all without reproach, and it will be given him. (ESV)

Being in God's will is where I want to stay. I love the following verse in the Amplified Bible:

Romans 12:2

And do not be conformed to this world [any longer with its superficial values and customs], but be transformed *and* progressively changed [as you mature spiritually] by the renewing of your mind [focusing on godly values and ethical attitudes], so that you may prove [for yourselves] what the will of God is, that which is good and acceptable and perfect [in His plan and purpose for you]. (AMP)

Additionally, even though I know when working toward goals the path from point A to point B is not usually a straight line, I want my path as straight as possible!

Proverbs 3:5-6

Trust in the Lord with all your heart, and do not lean on your own understanding. In all your ways acknowledge him, and he will make straight your paths. (ESV)

2. Write your goals down.

Science has proven that writing goals down makes a big difference. One way writing goals helps us achieve them is by a process called the "generation effect." People demonstrate better memory for things they have created or generated. Simply creating a goal taps into the generation effect. Then, when you write your goal down, you naturally process it on a deeper cognitive level, which in essence, is regenerating your goal and tapping into the generation effect twice. This solidifies your goal into your brain.[4]

I love when science proves the wisdom of the Bible as shown in the following verse:

Habakkuk 2:2

And the Lord answered me: "Write the vision; make it plain on tablets, so he may run who reads it." (ESV)

When we write down our goals, they become a tangible reality that we can begin to run toward.

Once you write your goals, post them where you can see them. Whether they are in your Bible, on your phone, on your mirror or in your car, if you see your goals and are reminded of them, you will have more success in reaching your goals.

3. Aim high.

This makes me think of the famous quote from author Norman Vincent Peale:

> *Shoot for the moon. Even if you miss, you'll land among the stars.*[5]

God wants us to aim higher and do bigger things than we can do in our own strength so that in the end, He will get the glory.

God-sized dreams are allowed. We have become scared to dream big because we fear failure. Sometimes we fear success. Maybe we do not want to be uncomfortable.

I believe we are created to dream big because we serve a big God. Our Creator has placed God-sized dreams within us. Nothing is impossible to those who believe (Mark 9:23). God wants us to aim higher and do things bigger than we can do in our own strength so that in the end, He will get the glory. Ephesians 3 confirms this.

Ephesians 3:20-21

Now to him who is able to do immeasurably more than all we ask or imagine, according to his power that is at work within us, to him be glory in the church and in Christ Jesus throughout all generations, for ever and ever! Amen. (NIV)

God-sized dreams are allowed. We have become scared to dream big because we fear failure. Sometimes we fear success. Maybe we do not want to be uncomfortable. To GROW we need to step out of our comfort zones.

4. <u>Make sure your goals do not contradict or conflict with each other.</u>

If you set a goal to start having the family over for lunch on Sundays, but also have a goal to serve at church in the new member classes which are held after Sunday service, you will have a conflict. Both goals cannot be achieved as written. To remedy this, either the family lunch needs to be on a different day, or you need to serve on a different team at church.

If you want to prioritize attending church every weekend but have a goal to advance at work to the weekend management position, these goals contradict since you will not be able to attend church if you get the promotion.

5. Set goals in each area of your life that are important to you.

Often if you are struggling in one area, it will lead to struggles in other areas. The converse is also true. If one area is thriving, it can bring that positivity into other areas. Take the time to know which areas are most important to you and have a clear vision of what you want each area to look like.

Common areas to write goals are:

- Physical Environment (Home or Office)
- Work/School
- Money/Finances
- Health and Wellness
- Family
- Relationships
- Spouse
- Personal Growth and Development
- Fun/Leisure/Recreation
- Spirituality
- Friendship
- Contentment
- Achievements/Successes
- Energy/Enthusiasm Level
- Emotional Health

6. Make sure your goals are written in the positive.

For example, instead of, "I will not eat sweets," make your goal, "I will eat five servings of fruit and vegetables a day."

By the way, positive goals work best just about everywhere. For example, when my son, Alexander, was little, he was very wiggly. If I were to bring him on an airplane, preemptively I may have said, "Do not kick the seat in front of you." This would leave him thinking about kicking the seat in front of him, and undoubtedly, the situation would not have ended well. If I told Alexander, "In planes we keep our feet on the floor," then it is likely he would not have even thought about the seat in front of him. He would have thought about keeping his feet on the floor. He is now so tall that when he is on a plane, he has to worry about his knees bothering the person in front of him.

7. <u>Make sure your goals match up with your core values.</u>

If your goals do not match up with your core values, your chances of success are diminished. Core values represent your beliefs and priorities. They drive all your decisions, choices, and actions. Become aware of them.

As a Christ-Follower, my faith is a core value. It is an unchangeable driving factor in all that I do. Every goal I create and every decision I make prayerfully goes through the filter of my faith.

8. <u>Get an accountability partner.</u>

If you are serious about reaching your goals, get serious about finding an accountability partner. This topic is important enough that it has its own chapter.

You want someone who is going to push you, encourage you, be tough with you when needed, and always speak truth. Research shows that accountability partners are instrumental in goal achievement.

> *The American Society of Training and Development found that people are 65 percent likely to meet a goal after committing to another person. Their chances of success increase to 95 percent when they build in ongoing meetings with their partners to check in on their progress.*[6]

9. <u>Make sure your goals are SMART.</u>

To set yourself up for success, when you are planning and creating goals, it is important to make sure your goals are SMART.

SMART

goals are:

Specific, Measurable, Action-oriented, Realistic, Time-bound

Be **SPECIFIC** with your goals. Ask *who, what, where, when, which, why.*

Example:

General Goal = "Read my Bible."

Specific Goal = "Read through the one-year Bible plan on my phone app each morning when I wake up."

Make your goal **MEASURABLE**. Make a goal plan. What are steps along the way? What do those steps look like? Identify the halfway mark. How much or how many? What will it look like when it is accomplished?

Example:

General Goal = "Lose weight."

Measurable Goal = "Lose 20 pounds by September 1st. Lose 10 of the pounds by May 1st."

Your goals need to be **ACTION ORIENTED.** A well written goal will move you to action so that you will reach it. Understanding the purpose, or the *why* behind your goal, is one way to achieve action. There were two thoughts that motivated me to action when I wrote this book—obedience to God's calling and a confidence that people will be positively impacted. These ideas got me out of bed in the morning, even when it was hard. Are you propelled toward your purpose with your goal? What moves you to action?

Additionally, have clearly defined steps which move you toward your goal. What actions need to happen to get you to the next step? Create actionable mile markers along the path toward your goal so you continue moving forward.

A goal should also be **REALISTIC**. Does the goal have enough priority in your life for you to put the time and effort into it? Have you considered potential obstacles? Is your goal aligned with the purpose God is calling you toward? If not, if may be unrealistic. Do you have what it takes to achieve it? Chances are a 5-foot-tall man will not make it as a player in the NBA. I have witnessed singing competitions where the participant's parent should have encouraged a new hobby long ago. It is painful to watch.

A goal can be large and realistic, but again, for success it must be important to you. Often big goals generate more excitement and motivation than smaller goals. I have seen this with sales professionals who will work ridiculously hard to be ranked at the top in sales to earn a nice vacation. They are not as likely to be excited and motivated if the payoff is only a trophy and bragging rights.

Having a **TIME BOUND** goal is important. Deadlines keep you focused and intentional. With a defined timeframe you are committed to reaching, success is more likely to be achieved. What will you accomplish by the end of next week? Next month? Next year?

The last tip for goal setting success is important and often overlooked.

10. Review and celebrate.

It is a good practice to take some time periodically to review your big picture: where you are, where you still want to go, and assess if changes need to be made. Often, once we have put our goals into practice for a while, they need to be tweaked. It is part of the journey and this is okay.

It is also important to reflect on successes and celebrate. Have you made it to the halfway point of a large goal? Acknowledge this achievement and take the time to celebrate. We are always learning and growing. Celebrating along the way encourages us to keep taking steps.

Sample goals for the topics covered in this book are scattered throughout the chapters to assist you when considering your own goals.

Now that we have reviewed ten tips for goal setting success and SMART goals, it is time to jump in, read each chapter, prayerfully consider the areas to focus on for growth, set some goals, and GROW.

NOTES ● THOUGHTS ● INSIGHTS

Comfort Zones

QUOTES ABOUT <u>COMFORT ZONES</u>

***The comfort zone is one of the greatest enemies of human potential.*[1]**

-Brian Tracy

***We have to be honest about what we want and take risks rather than lie to ourselves and make excuses to stay in our comfort zone.*[2]**

-Roy T. Bennett

***A ship in harbor is safe, but that is not what ships are built for.*[3]**

-John A. Shedd

Chapter 1

Comfort Zones

Growth happens outside of your comfort zone.

For growth to take place, we need to get uncomfortable and I believe being uncomfortable is where the fun begins!

In this chapter we are going to define comfort zones, explore the obstacles that keep us inside of our comfort zones, check out some tips for stepping out of our comfort zones, and look to Jesus as our example. My hope is that you will be inspired to get a little uncomfortable and GROW.

COMFORT ZONES DEFINED

A comfort zone is a place where you feel safe. It is a stress-free zone. In your comfort zone you are in control and you are at ease.

I want to be clear that I am not against comfort zones. We all need comfort zones. I hope your home feels like a comfort zone to you. I hope you have a comfy chair to sit in and a nice fluffy pillow to lay your head upon. If you love to fish, a comfort zone may be your boat. Diving into your hobby can be like diving into a comfort zone, whether biking, running, reading, woodworking or painting. It is wonderful to have a stress-free place in which to escape, where you can refuel, refresh, regroup, and spend time with God. If you do not have a comfort zone, I encourage you to create one.

Once we have spent time in our comfort zones, we need to get intentional about leaving our comfort zones on a regular basis. In my experience, people do not like to leave their comfort zones, because, well...it is uncomfortable! The thing is, we are all purpose-filled individuals. God created each one of us with a unique purpose which will look like no one else's purpose. We have Kingdom work to do. To accomplish what God is calling us to do requires leaving our comfort zone.

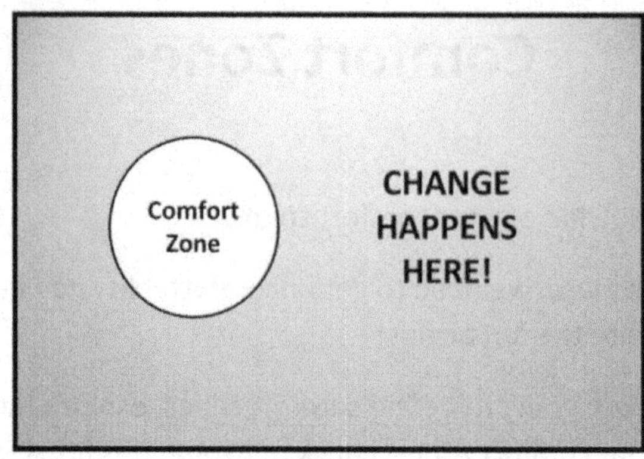

Change happens when we step out of our comfort zones. Change can be positive or negative. Sometimes we choose change, and sometimes it is thrust upon us. Every time we face a change, it is an opportunity for growth. We cannot grow without change. For example, if we desire to GROW closer to God with a morning devotional time, we may need to set the alarm and wake up earlier to have focused quiet time. This change in schedule can be difficult. If we want to declutter our homes, it may be uncomfortable to let go of some of our stuff that we have held onto for years, but the result will be positive when we have a more peaceful home. If we decide to improve our health, it will require change in diet and exercise to get results.

When we do not proactively choose growth, change will still occur, but we may not get the results we desire. If I choose to ignore the condition of my home or ignore my health, it will continue to get worse. The ramifications of not starting my day connecting with God are tremendous. I will not be effective with the Kingdom work I am created to accomplish!

Sample Comfort Zones Goal

I will schedule lunch with Uncle John next week to share my testimony with him.

Our daily choices to step out of our comfort zones make the difference between a mediocre life and one lived with excellence.

Our daily choices to step out of our comfort zones make the difference between a mediocre life and one lived with excellence.

Sometimes it is hard to see that change is needed. A friend stopped by the other day and I had on my black fuzzy house slippers. She looked at them and immediately said, "Rachelle, it may be time for you to get a new pair of slippers." My old worn out slippers were comfortable. I did not realize change was needed. When I looked at my slippers with a fresh perspective, I could indeed see my friend was right. They were torn, had paint splatters on them, and were very dingy. Change was definitely needed!

I have seen this with my clients. They are bored with their job. Their job has become like comfortable, worn out slippers. But the prospect of having to change is hard! The flip side is that the same old thing happening every day gets boring. When you get to the point where you are no longer challenged or can do it with your eyes closed, then you are not growing. To leave the known and go into the unknown can be hard and scary, but it can also be fun and exhilarating. At some point a choice has to be made—do I stay or do I GROW? Are there areas in your life where you have become too comfortable?

CHANGE HAPPENS!

In reality, there are very few things in life that will occur 100% of the time. Here is my list:

1. Death (Last I checked, there was a 100% mortality rate.)
2. Change

Whether you are excited by change, or would rather stick with the status quo, it is important to understand that change is an inevitable part of our lives.

I am sure there is more that can be added to the list, but I think this sums it up. Everything else I came up with can fall under change (the seasons, taxes, my weight, etc.). In fact, death itself could fall under change.

Why does the word "change" invoke fear in so many people? How can we get to a point where we accept the change that will inevitably come into our lives? Maybe we need to understand it more before we learn to embrace it.

The definition of *change* is:

1. to make the form, nature, content, future course, etc., of (something) different from what it is or from what it would be if left alone
2. to transform or convert[4]

People vary in reaction to this definition. Some cling to the part of the definition that says *left alone*— "Just leave me alone!" I personally tend to get bored easily and like change. Whether you are excited by change, or would rather stick with the status quo, it is important to accept that change is an inevitable part of life. I want to encourage you to embrace it. We can choose to take change by the horns instead of becoming victims of change.

I have yet to find a person who does not think some part of their life would be improved with change.

Let's learn more about change. There are three types of change we will encounter in our lives. Here they are with some examples:

1. Lifestyle Changes
    - Health/Diet/Exercise
    - Limit or end toxic relationships
    - Tackle addictions (smoking, drugs, pornography, etc.)

- Limit media time
- Increase spiritual disciplines

2. Major Life Changes
    - Graduation
    - Marriage/Divorce
    - Job Change/Retirement
    - New baby
    - Relocation
    - Empty nest
    - Death of a loved one

3. Internal Changes
    - Underlying beliefs about oneself (not good enough, not smart enough, too fat)
    - Fear
    - Outlook or perspective shift
    - Emotional intelligence *(definition on page 40*)

This list reminds me that there is a time for everything under heaven (Ecclesiastes 3). Further reflection reveals that sometimes we can choose when the change will take place, sometimes we cannot. Regardless of how change happens, change equals an opportunity for growth.

Change equals an opportunity for growth.

If we are going to choose to live a purpose-filled life with intentionality, then we must view change as our ally.

WHAT IS EMOTIONAL INTELLIGENCE?

A person's Emotional Intelligence (EI) or Emotional Quotient(EQ) is derived from 5 areas: **Self-Awareness** (the ability to recognize your moods, emotions and motivators), **Self-Regulation** (the ability to control your moods, emotions; to be able to think before acting), **Motivation** (driving passion outside of money or status), **Empathy** (the ability to recognize other's moods, emotions and motivators) and **Social Skills** (ability to manage relationships, rapport and build networks).[5] Growth in Emotional Intelligence produces emotional maturity.

As a Christ-Follower it is important to understand that spiritual health correlates to Emotional Intelligence. Some examples of this are: our *motivation* will be greatly derived from our God-given purpose or calling, our faith calls us to have *empathy* toward others, and we need to have the *social skills* to develop healthy relationships with others to impact the Kingdom.

Let's look again at the second definition of change:

Change - To be transformed

This definition makes me think about caterpillars and butterflies. Our comfort zone is our cocoon. Are you stuck in your cocoon? There are beautiful things waiting for you once you embrace change.

"To be transformed" brings these Scriptures to mind:

2 Corinthians 3:18

And we all, who with unveiled faces contemplate the Lord's glory, are being transformed into his image with ever-increasing glory, which comes from the Lord, who is the Spirit. (NIV)

Romans 12:2

Do not conform to the pattern of this world, but be transformed by the renewing of your mind. Then you will be able to test and approve what God's will is—his good, pleasing and perfect will. (NIV)

When we prayerfully consider our next chapter and set goals for growth, we can step into the purpose we were created to fulfill.

Change is a natural and healthy part of the Christian walk.

Our lives, like a book, are made up of many chapters. Change comes along whether we want it to or not, and then we are faced with a new chapter of life opening before us. If we live a life of intentionality, then we will look at this blank chapter with excitement and embrace the opportunity to write it how we choose. As a Christ-Follower, we can invite the Holy Spirit to guide us. When we prayerfully consider our next chapter and set goals for growth, we can step into the purpose we were created to fulfill. How exciting is that?

Or we can choose not to choose. That is a choice! Mistakes and stumbles are better than regrets and what ifs. Often the discomfort of stepping out of our comfort zones can result in hoorays and hallelujahs. When you look back on your life's book, will you be pleased?

JUST ONE STEP

To reach our goals, we need to continue to take steps outside of our comfort zones. It does not have to be drastic to grow—just little, planned, incremental steps. Take snow skiing for example. The first time you put on skis, it is uncomfortable. You play around on a bunny hill until you figure it out. You then take the next step to a green slope. The first time you go down a green slope, it may be scary. The twentieth time you go down a green slope will be easy. It may even get boring. To grow as a skier, you choose to advance to the next level and try a blue slope. With each little step, we grow. Another example can be found in teaching a child to read. Initially, they learn the letters of the alphabet and their sounds. Next, they are introduced to easy readers. Eventually they will move on to chapter books. Just one little step at a time, and you will have success. We just need to choose to take a step.

Step by step we can accomplish the big things we are called by God to do.

With the gift of hindsight, we can often see how God brought us through steps to prepare us for something bigger. This book is an example of that. Writing a book was not initially something I set out to do. God brought me through steps which prepared me to write. First, God placed a passion in my heart for helping Christ-Followers GROW. I created a basic "Christian-Walk Assessment Tool" and used this tool to speak to groups about goal setting in areas of faith. He then gave me the idea to start a GROW study group where several of us gathered to look through different areas of Christianity with the purpose of growing and encouraging each other. As the leader, I researched different topics to present. After a year of doing this topical research, God put the idea of a book on my heart, and I already had much of the content developed.

If I had set out to write a book years ago, I would not have been ready, and it would have been an overwhelming project. It would have been like trying to ski a black slope, or like having a kindergartener read a college text—I would have been unprepared and probably crashed along the way.

Step by step we can accomplish the big things we are called by God to do.

WHAT KEEPS US IN OUR COMFORT ZONE?

If you ask people if they want to grow and improve their lives, they will answer, "Yes!" But often, they still get stuck. I have identified nine ways my clients get stuck and are kept from impacting the world outside their comfort zones instead of moving into their "GROW zone."

Sample Comfort Zones Goal

I am signing up for the mission trip to India that the Holy Spirit has been nudging me to do.

OBSTACLES TO LEAVING OUR COMFORT ZONES

1. Fear

Satan commonly uses fear to stop us in our tracks. God knew it would be a ploy of the enemy, so He has given us many Scriptures to combat fear. Here are two of my favorites:

Joshua 1:9

Have I not commanded you? Be strong and courageous. Do not be frightened, and do not be dismayed, for the Lord your God is with you wherever you go. (ESV)

2 Timothy 1:7

For God has not given us a spirit of fear, but of power and of love and of a sound mind. (NKJV)

Often people have fear in one of these areas:

a. Fear of Failure - People do not like to fail, yet it is unrealistic to believe that we will never mess up. A perspective change on this is helpful. The truth is, we do not fail unless we quit. Thomas Edison had thousands of failed attempts at creating a light bulb before he was successful.[6] Michael Jordon, arguably the greatest basketball player of all time, said this:

> *I've missed more than 9,000 shots in my career. I've lost almost 300 games. 26 times I've been trusted to take the game winning shot and missed. I've failed over and over and over again in my life, and that is why I succeed.*[7]

Our mistakes and mess-ups are learning opportunities for growth.

b. Fear of Success - Sometimes people are terrified of the results of success. Will they be put in the limelight? Can they handle the success? Some people feel they are not good enough to succeed or they do not deserve success, which is believing a lie.

c. Fear of the Unknown - The truth is, all our tomorrows are unknown. Are you a worst-case scenario kind of person, always dreading the future? Only God knows our tomorrows. We are called to live in the present.

Besides fear, another way I see my clients get stuck in their comfort zones is when they struggle with perfectionism.

2. Perfectionism

Perfectionism is the need to appear perfect. People who struggle with perfectionism often have unrealistic expectations for themselves and judge themselves harshly for not meeting the unrealistic expectations. Perfectionism can also paralyze people into inaction. Often people will stay in their comfort zones because they know they cannot be perfect, so they do not even make an attempt. Your journey is about progress, not perfection. We all fall short and there are no perfect humans. The goal is to GROW. In fact, it is wise to expect that you will mess up along the way. It is okay. Life is messy. When planning our goals, remember that the path from point A to point B is usually not a straight line. It will be filled with the ups and downs of life. Just keep striving toward your goal. Commit that you will not allow yourself to be paralyzed by perfectionism. Instead, let's strive for excellence.

> Our mistakes and mess-ups are learning opportunities for growth.

3. <u>Lack of Motivation</u>

Motivation can come externally (rewards or punishment) or internally (purpose, passion, enjoyment, self-satisfaction). I love seeing when people are passionate about their purpose. Nothing will stop them. They wake up excited to jump out of bed and out of their comfort zones to get started. What motivates you to step out of your comfort zone?

> Your journey is about progress, not perfection.

4. <u>Poor Habits</u>

A habit is something we do routinely, often without much thought put into it. An example of poor habits is watching too much TV or spending too much time surfing the Internet. These things keep us inside our comfort zones. Become aware of the empty time-zappers in your life and choose to start taking steps to minimize them.

Sample Comfort Zones Goal

*Although I have never led before,
I will step up to lead a Bible study for
the ladies in my neighborhood.*

5. Isolation

We are not meant to do life alone. Not only will being around the right kind of people encourage us, it may also be where we discover our purpose.

6. We Believe Lies

Satan will tell you anything to get you to stay in your comfort zone. Know the truth about who you are in Christ and what God has called you to do. Be aware of your thoughts and shut the door on the enemy and his lies.

7. Self-Doubt

God does not call the qualified, He qualifies the called. All you have to be is a willing vessel. Do not doubt that God can use you.

8. Laziness

An object at rest tends to stay at rest. It is time to get moving. The Bible says much on this subject:

Proverbs 6:9-11

How long will you lie there, O sluggard? When will you arise from your sleep? A little sleep, a little slumber, a little folding of the hands to rest, and poverty will come upon you like a robber, and want like an armed man. (ESV)

9. Stuck in the Past

We cannot move forward if we are looking backward. Your past does not define you. Learn what you need from your past, then leave your past behind. Move forward into the purpose God has for your life. Be focused on today and trust God with tomorrow. Yesterday cannot be changed.

BREAKING FREE FROM OUR COMFORT ZONES

How do we overcome the obstacles that keep us in our comfort zones? Here are seven ways to propel us out of our comfort zones and into our purpose:

1. Pray.

Ask the Holy Spirit to guide you on the path He has for you, and then take a step of obedience towards God's plan for your life.

Psalm 32:8

I will instruct you and teach you in the way you should go;
I will counsel you with my loving eye on you. (NIV)

2. Identify your fear.

Knowledge is power. Often Satan will use the same tricks over and over to stop us from reaching our destiny. Write down your favorite Scriptures about fear and speak them out loud.

3. Embrace failure.

If we change our perspective on failure and see it as an ally to growth, then we will see failure as a stepping stone toward reaching our goals.

Proverbs 24:16

For the righteous falls seven times and rises again, but the wicked stumble in times of calamity. (ESV)

4. Surround yourself with risk-takers.

If everyone around you looks at you like you are crazy when you step out of your comfort zone, then you will be less likely to step out. Look for friends who will drag you out of your comfort zone and encourage you to keep taking steps. Look at these Scriptures for inspiration:

Proverbs 13:20

Whoever walks with the wise becomes wise, but the companion of fools will suffer harm. (ESV)

Proverbs 12:26

The righteous choose their friends carefully, but the way of the wicked leads them astray. (NIV)

5. Remind yourself of the benefits of stepping out of your comfort zone.

We all want to GROW. We all want to make a difference, be a good example, and live the best lives we can. Keep your eye on the prize.

Philippians 3:13-14

Brothers, I do not consider that I have made it my own. But one thing I do: forgetting what lies behind and straining forward to what lies ahead, I press on toward the goal for the prize of the upward call of God in Christ Jesus. (ESV)

6. Be persistent.

Just like the squeaky wheel gets the grease, persistence will eventually pay off. Keep taking steps in the direction God is calling you. Commit to yourself that you will get back up again and again.

7. Rely on God's Word for courage.

Choose your favorite courage verses and write them down, memorize them, and speak them out loud. God's Word is the Sword of the Spirit (Ephesians 6:17). Use it to pierce through your comfort zone bubble.

JESUS AS OUR EXAMPLE

Jesus' life is the ultimate example of stepping out of a comfort zone. He left heaven! He left the beauty and splendor of heaven to become a helpless baby knowing He would die a horrible death—a death that paid the penalty for our sins even though He Himself was sinless.

I started thinking about examples from the Bible of people who God called out of comfort zones. There are so many!

Abram, Moses, Joshua, David, Esther, the twelve disciples, Paul...the list goes on. Our heroes of faith made a difference when they stepped out in faith, stepped out of their comfort zones, and obeyed God.

Our heroes of faith made a difference when they stepped out in faith, stepped out of their comfort zones, and obeyed God.

On the flip side, when David became too comfortable and stayed home from battle, things went horribly wrong. He ended up committing adultery and had a man murdered.

Esther is a great story to use as an illustration of stepping out of comfort zones. It took a lot of prayer and bravery for Esther to approach the king, for which she could have been killed.

Esther 4:16

"Go, gather all the Jews to be found in Susa, and hold a fast on my behalf, and do not eat or drink for three days, night or day. I and my young women will also fast as you do. Then, I will go to the king, though it is against the law, and if I perish, I perish." (ESV)

Because Esther was willing to step out of her comfort zone, the Jewish people were saved from annihilation.

Another comfort zone illustration can be found with Peter walking on water, which is my favorite Bible story for the topic of comfort zones.

Matthew 14:27-31

But Jesus immediately said to them: "Take courage! It is I. Don't be afraid."
"Lord, if it's you," Peter replied, "tell me to come to you on the water."
"Come," he said.
Then Peter got down out of the boat, walked on the water and came toward Jesus. But when he saw the wind, he was afraid and, beginning to sink, cried out, "Lord, save me!"
Immediately Jesus reached out his hand and caught him. "You of little faith," he said, "why did you doubt?" (NIV)

People want to focus on the fact that Peter started to sink, but I love the fact that he had enough faith to step out of the boat.

What an amazing example of stepping out of a comfort zone into the unknown. It was dark and windy with crashing waves, and yet Peter fixed his eyes on Jesus and his faith took over. He accomplished something no other apostle did—he walked on water. People want to focus on the fact that Peter started to sink, but I love the fact that he had enough faith to step out of the boat.

If you could pick, which disciple would you be in this story? I believe most would choose Peter.

We all would love to experience walking on water, but that requires us to lean into our faith and trust God. When we step out of our comfort zones, we will create our own "walking on water" stories. Christianity is not for wimps. Often we have to do it scared, but God promises that He is with us and will never leave us.

God has created each of us with a purpose—a purpose specifically designed for us to accomplish. We must get over our fears, over our laziness, over whatever is holding us back from our destinies. We may have to do it scared. And just like a roller coaster, life can be an exhilarating experience. Our Christian walk will be full of ups and downs. You may not know what is past the next curve on the ride we call life, and like a roller coaster, you may be thrown for a loop or two! I do not want to be on the bench watching others. I am jumping onboard. Come join me!

When we step out of our comfort zones, we will create our own "walking on water" stories.

HEART CHECK

The purpose of stepping out of our comfort zones is change. As a Christ-Follower, we want to grow more and more like Christ. If we do our part—pray, plan, take action—at the end of the day we can rest, knowing we are on the path God has called us.

I want to encourage you. Like Peter, maybe it is time to get your feet wet. Just take one step and keep your eyes on Jesus. It can be fun and exciting. It can be scary. But what if you do not get out of the boat? God has a purpose for your life. Grab hold of it.

What are you being called to that is uncomfortable?

Maybe it is waking up before the sun to have quiet time with God. Maybe you are being called to speak to a friend who is not living wisely. Maybe it is taking the time to listen to someone who needs to be heard. Maybe it is taking a new path in your career. These actions may seem small but each action has the potential to be a world changer.

Wherever the Holy Spirit is prompting you to GROW, now is the perfect time to take a step. Stop waiting and start acting. You only have one life–please make the most of it. In what ways do you want your world to change?

Could you imagine if all Christ-Followers chose to follow God outside of their comfort zones? The impact would be amazing! Be a part of this. Join in. This is a choice you have to make.

Where is your next step going to take you?

COACH CORNER

Jessie has been a client for years. In her prayer and journaling time, she felt like God gave her a vision to reach professional women through a private group that meets monthly. This idea overwhelmed her, and she did not feel qualified. She would have to step out of her comfort zone. It was going to be hard to create, hard to advertise, and hard to gain traction. Through coaching, she began to realize that God was calling her to make this a ministry with the potential to positively impact the lives of women and help them grow. Together we created a plan for her to bring her idea to fruition. Step by step she made progress. When she would become overwhelmed with the big picture, we would review the purpose of the group she was creating. I always encouraged her to just take the next step. Eventually it was time to launch the group. She sent out invitations, terrified that no one would be interested. People came! The group continues to grow and impact women to be their best.

*To enhance your learning experience, scan the QR Code or visit **AnEncouragedLife.com** to watch the supplemental video for this chapter.*

COMFORT ZONES VIDEO LESSON

1. ____________________________ happens outside of your comfort zone.

2. Change equals an opportunity for ________________________________.

3. When we prayerfully consider our next steps and set goals for

   growth, we can step into the ___________________________________ we were created to fulfill.

4. ______________________________ can keep us inside our comfort zones.

5. The perfect time to take a step toward growth is __________________.

COMFORT ZONES
DISCUSSION QUESTIONS

10
9
8
7
6
5
4
3
2
1

1. On a scale from 1-10, where do you rank your current satisfaction in the area of Comfort Zones? Color in the scale to the right.
2. Share a time when you were in an uncomfortable situation. How did you grow from this experience?
3. Change is defined on page 38. What aspect of the definition personally challenged you?
4. Of the nine obstacles to leaving comfort zones found on pages 43-47, which ones impact you the most? Why?
5. If you knew you could not fail, what would you do? How can you overcome what is stopping you from accomplishing this goal?
6. Of the seven ways to break free from your comfort zones on pages 47-48, which one(s) were most helpful to you? Why?
7. What would growth in the area of Comfort Zones look like for you?
8. What is the most important thing you have learned on the topic of Comfort Zones?
9. If Comfort Zones is an area in which you feel prompted by the Holy Spirit to GROW, write a SMART goal below. Describe what this area looks like to you right now, so you can look back and measure growth.

SMART

goals are:

Specific, Measurable, Action-oriented, Realistic, Time-bound

NOTES ● THOUGHTS ● INSIGHTS

Simplicity

QUOTES ABOUT SIMPLICITY

***We buy things we don't need with money we don't have to impress people we don't like.*[1]**

-Dave Ramsey

***Simple can be harder than complex:
You have to work hard to get your thinking clean to make it simple.
But it's worth it in the end because once you get there,
you can move mountains.*[2]**

-Steve Jobs

***I do believe in simplicity. It is astonishing as well as sad, how many trivial affairs even the wisest thinks he must attend to in a day; how singular an affair he thinks he must omit.*[3]**

-Henry David Thoreau

Chapter 2

Simplicity

Simplicity should be simple, right?

That is what I thought until I started researching this topic. It rocked my world! Many of us have a tendency to make things more complicated than they have to be. At least I do, that is for sure.

We are going to talk about simplicity in our surroundings, our schedules, our minds, and our speech. We will also look at some tips for managing complicated people. When we simplify, we will more easily be able to focus on our purpose, set goals, and ultimately GROW in our relationship with God.

SIMPLICITY DEFINED

Simplicity, simply put, is putting God above all else. Simplicity is focusing on God instead of on stuff. It is being intentional about decluttering our lives and our minds so we have more room for God.

The following verse is interesting when we consider simplicity:

Matthew 6:31-33

Therefore do not be anxious, saying, 'What shall we eat?' or 'What shall we drink?' or 'What shall we wear?' For the Gentiles seek after all these things, and your heavenly Father knows that you need them all. But seek first the kingdom of God and his righteousness, and all these things will be added to you. (ESV)

Simplicity is focusing on God instead of on stuff. It is being intentional about decluttering our lives and our minds so we have more room for God.

I love that this Scripture says to seek God *first*.

When we simplify our lives, we remove all the extra things and all the extra thoughts that are weighing us down, robbing us of our energy, stealing our time and keeping us from our purpose. The amazing thing is, when we put God first and trust Him, we do not have to be anxious or worried.

God's got this!

Sample Simplicity Goal:

I will spend 10 minutes per day decluttering my home/office.

When packing for an overnight trip, some people may take just a little backpack: "All I need is an extra shirt with a toothbrush and a few toiletries. I'll just wear the same jeans again—no big deal."

But others need a very large suitcase for an overnight trip: "What if I end up needing something nicer? What if the hotel's hair dryer is broken? And how can I possibly know today what shoes I will feel like wearing tomorrow?"

You know those people. In fact, you may identify with them. They wear themselves out lugging around all their baggage.

All our stuff weighs us down, slows us down, distracts us, and takes up our precious time and energy.

We as a society are weighed down by our stuff—both our possessions and the stuff inside our heads. We worry and are anxious because of our stuff or the want for more stuff.

When we have cluttered homes, cluttered desks, cluttered schedules, and cluttered minds, we are not at our best. It is harder to hear God amid all the distractions.

CLUTTERED SURROUNDINGS

I confess that I tend to have a cluttered home. When my kids were little, I taught them "stash and dash" techniques so that we could have the main areas of my home "company ready" in 10-15 minutes—as long as company did not want to look in my bedroom or closets! We have too much stuff and this is an area in which I am slowly improving. With the help of my own Life Coach, I have made progress in this area. Housework is not a high priority for me, and I will not beat myself up if it is less than perfect, but I am moving forward towards simplicity. When you are working on goals, give yourself plenty of grace. We are aiming for progress, not perfection.

When we have cluttered homes, cluttered desks, cluttered schedules, and cluttered minds, we are not at our best. It is harder to hear God amid all the distractions.

Often people have cluttered surroundings because they see value in everything. Sometimes it comes from a scarcity mindset brought on by fear. I come from a long line of cluttered homes and would love to believe that it is hereditary, although I know it is not. Much of what I used to battle is perfectionism. I could not make it perfect, so I did not try at all.

On the other side of the spectrum are the people with "museum" houses. Their homes are so clean, nothing is out of place. I have been to homes where I am scared to allow my children to sit on the sofa because they might wrinkle it.

I believe it is healthiest to fall somewhere in the middle on this spectrum. If your home is too cluttered, it could hinder your relationship with God for reasons such as: being overwhelmed by your surroundings, being disappointed in yourself, or not having enough peace and order to be conducive to connecting with God. On the other hand, if you are so busy trying to keep your home perfect, it could also be hard to slow it down enough to have quality time with God. Balance is key. It comes down to the heart.

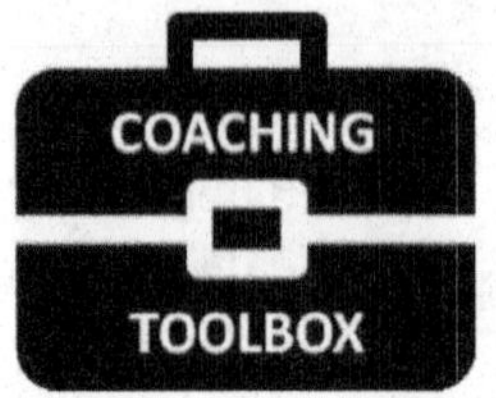

Everybody Needs a Professional Life Coach

The best of the best have coaches. Michael Phelps and Tom Brady have coaches. Fortune 100 CEOs have coaches. If you want to get serious about being your best while growing and improving in all areas of your life, then I believe you need a Life Coach. Whether you want to improve as a mom, a business owner, or a Christ-Follower, in whatever area you want to grow—with a professional Life Coach you will achieve your goals. I have a Life Coach because I want to be my best, too.

> We over-commit. We fill our lives with so much good that we do not have time for God.

CLUTTERED SCHEDULES

People often have a tendency to overcommit. We fill our lives with so much good that we do not have time for God. We feel like we cannot possibly say no. We want to do it all, see it all, be it all for everyone. We are living such busy, fast-paced lives.

As parents, we want our kids to have *all* the opportunities, so we sign them up for everything. We bring them on *all* the fieldtrips. We go to *all* the events. Maybe jumping in puddles is okay rather than going to the water park. Kids do not have time for the simpler things in life anymore—nor do the adults. We go, go, go. We plan vacations that are jam-packed. We come back from our vacations needing a vacation.

Cluttered, complicated schedules are exhausting. Are you tired of the pace? It does not have to be this way. Maybe it is time to simplify.

A healthy life has margin. To live optimally, we need wiggle room in our schedules. Every minute of every day does not need to be scheduled. We must be intentional about creating margin in our lives. If this book had no margins on the sides of the pages, you would find it hard to read. When filling a glass, you leave space at the top rather than filling it all the way to the brim; otherwise, it will spill over and make a mess. The same is true with our surroundings, our schedules, and our minds, which we will talk about next. What do you do to ensure you have margin in your life?

Sample Simplicity Goal:

When asked to volunteer,
I will seek God and pray before putting
another commitment on my calendar.

CLUTTERED MINDS

Our modern culture has information overload. We are constantly bombarded with stuff to mentally process. This information overload coupled with our fast-paced schedules leads to cluttered minds. We multi-task, have mental checklists for our checklists colliding in our heads, then end up having trouble sleeping because we cannot turn off our brains at night. For example, at any given moment, multiple thoughts could be swirling around my brain simultaneously:

"What is the deadline for that application?"

"Do avocados have protein?"

"Will I make it to the gas station to fill up my car?"

"I want to text that article to Jessie."

When my mind is going at such a fast pace, I am unlikely to hear God's whispers.

When my mind is going at such a fast pace, I am not likely to hear God's whispers.

Additionally, people will clutter their minds with lies and second guesses. We can easily become critical of ourselves with a negative internal dialog. Here are some examples:

"I look fat in this outfit."

"I'm stupid."

"Why did I say that?"

"I do not fit in."

We become our own worst enemy. Actually, these thoughts come from the enemy—Satan, who is always trying to stop us in our tracks and keep us from our purpose! We have to train ourselves to distinguish the lies and then focus only on the truth.

Often when I meet with a coaching client, we will brainstorm solutions. Here are some ideas to get you thinking about solutions regarding a cluttered mind.

5 TIPS FOR DECLUTTERING OUR MINDS

1. Write your thoughts down.

Keep a notebook or journal nearby to put the thoughts in your head onto paper. When you know you will not forget something, you can stop worrying about it. Additionally, when you write your thoughts down, you can get clarity by prayerfully considering what is most important. Then, you are easily able to prioritize your next steps.

2. Choose.

When we put off making decisions, we end up carrying all the indecisions in our mind. Do not second guess yourself. Make your choice then move on so that you can clear your brain of pending decisions.

3. Focus.

People sometimes pride themselves on being able to multitask, but when we allow ourselves to focus on one thing at a time, we train our minds to only focus on what is in front of us. We clear the brain clutter because we know we will get to the other things later. Often with this concentrated focus, we are more effective. The ability to focus on God with an unjumbled mind is a powerful way to GROW in our relationship with Him.

4. Live in the present.

Do not waste your energy worrying about the past. You cannot change it. Learn from it and then move on. In the same way, worrying about tomorrow is a lot of wasted time and energy. We need to learn to stop worrying and focus on today.

Philippians 3:13-14

Brothers and sisters, I do not consider myself yet to have taken hold of it. But one thing I do: Forgetting what is behind and straining toward what is ahead, I press on toward the goal to win the prize for which God has called me heavenward in Christ Jesus. (NIV)

Matthew 6:34

Therefore do not be anxious about tomorrow, for tomorrow will be anxious for itself. Sufficient for the day is its own trouble. (ESV)

5. Have check-ups.

Become aware of your thoughts. Is your mind racing? What can you do about it? Get into the habit of routinely doing thought checks and practice clearing the clutter.

The ability to focus on God with an unjumbled mind is a powerful way to GROW in our relationship with Him.

It is hard to hear God when we have cluttered minds. If our goal is to grow in our relationship with Him, then we need to consider setting goals toward simplifying our thoughts.

HEART CHECK

Simplicity really comes down to the heart. If we are seeking God first, and trusting Him, we will be able to let go of things that are not needed and begin living a simpler, more peaceful life.

It is important to periodically examine our hearts. Does having a lack of simplicity in your life keep you from growing in your relationship with God? Consider this Scripture:

> Eliminating *stuff* without filling the space with God will not get the desired results of choosing simplicity. Remember, it is a matter of the heart.

Matthew 6:19-21

Do not lay up for yourselves treasures on earth, where moth and rust destroy and where thieves break in and steal, but lay up for yourselves treasures in heaven, where neither moth nor rust destroys and where thieves do not break in and steal. For where your treasure is, there your heart will be also. (ESV)

And yet, life can so easily, so quickly get complicated.

It may be time to simplify.

Here is another thought. What if our pursuit for more is really a lack of faith in God's provision? Do we tell ourselves, "I've got this, God"?

Society elevates people by what they can accumulate. He who has the most toys wins! Large homes, closets full of designer clothes, fancy cars—these things become how we define success if we are not careful. If our ambition and industry are not rooted in God, then neither will amount to anything in the end. When we are living out our God-given purpose, our perspective of what is important will shift. What does success for a Christ-Follower look like? What does success look like to you?

> Are you pursuing God with your whole heart, or are you pursuing wealth, or comfort or something else? Who or what is first?

To take it further, the idea or desire for a simple lifestyle must not come before God. For example, we can buy a tiny house, sell our possessions, live off the land, etc., but as we declutter and make space, we need to be intentional about filling that space with God.

Eliminating *stuff* without filling the space with God will not get the desired results of choosing simplicity. Simplicity is a matter of the heart.

Are you pursuing God with your whole heart or are you pursuing wealth or comfort or something else? Who or what is first? I am reminded of this verse:

Luke 16:13

No servant can serve two masters; for either he will hate the one and love the other, or else he will be loyal to the one and despise the other. You cannot serve God and mammon. (NKJV)

WHAT DO WE DO WITH COMPLICATED PEOPLE?

We have all dealt with complicated people. Maybe we have even been those complicated people. My hope is that this chapter will help us become less complicated. But what do we do with our friends and family that have not benefitted from these truths about simplicity? Since we all have to manage complicated people at times, here are some helpful tips.

SIX TIPS FOR MANAGING COMPLICATED PEOPLE

1. Set clear boundaries.

Boundaries are critical when it comes to managing difficult or complicated people. If allowed, complicated people will zap your time, drain you and add stress to your life. A sample boundary would be letting them know that evening is family time and you do not take phone calls or respond to texts after six o'clock. Set the rules and remind them if necessary. Otherwise, they could potentially hinder your growth and detract from your goals and purpose.

2. Be strong.

Oftentimes, complicated people will use tactics like offense, pouting, anger, or the silent treatment to get their way. Be aware of these manipulative tactics and stand your ground. You are not responsible for their emotions.

3. Stay calm.

Do not let complicated people push your buttons. Listen and then prayerfully consider if you will respond. When you do respond, respond in love instead of a knee-jerk reaction.

4. Pick your battles.

You always have the choice to decide if you will engage with a complicated person. Sometimes it may be wiser not to take part in what they are doing.

5. Eliminate or minimize.

The majority of the people you surround yourself with (in your inner circle) should uplift you, encourage you, and help you become your best. It may be time to begin distancing yourself from those who continuously drain you. Some people are only meant to be in your life for a season. Prayerfully consider who surrounds you. This brings me to our final tip for managing complicated people.

6. Pray.

Ask the Holy Spirit to guide you and give you grace to manage this area of your life.

JESUS AS OUR EXAMPLE

It is humbling to look at Jesus as an example in this area as we strive to be more like Him. Jesus was homeless and possessionless for much of His time in ministry. In today's world, it would be akin to couch surfing.

Luke 9:58

Jesus said to him, "Foxes have holes, and birds of the air have nests, but the Son of Man has nowhere to lay his head." (ESV)

When His disciples followed Him, they did not even take a backpack.

Mark 6:8-9

He charged them to take nothing for their journey except a staff—no bread, no bag, no money in their belts—but to wear sandals and not put on two tunics. (ESV)

Do we all need to be homeless to be more Christ-like? I do not think so. Some of Jesus's followers had wealth and status like Joseph of Arimathea, who used his wealth and position to serve the Kingdom for Jesus' burial.

Matthew 27:57-60

When it was evening, there came a rich man from Arimathea, named Joseph, who also was a disciple of Jesus. He went to Pilot and asked for the body of Jesus. Then Pilate ordered it to be given to Him. And Joseph took the body and wrapped it in a clean linen shroud and laid it in his own new tomb, which he had cut in the rock And he rolled a great stone to the entrance of the tomb and went away.

It all comes down to one question: What are you pursuing *first*?

Sample Simplicity Goal

I will remove social media apps from my phone and only check them one time per day on another device. I will use the freed up time to seek God at least two times per day by Bible reading, listening to worship music, or prayer.

SIMPLIFY OUR SPEECH

So far, we have talked about simplifying our surroundings, our schedules, and our minds. We have looked at our hearts, managing complicated people, and explored Jesus' life as an example of simplicity. Next, let's look at simplifying our speech.

It used to drive my kids crazy when I answered their requests with, "Maybe." Maybes are complicated answers that left them in limbo. *Will it be yes or no? How long will it take her to get back with us?* In hindsight, if I really needed to consider my answer before responding, it would have been better to say, "Let me pray about that and I will get back with you tomorrow." It was important to follow up with them the next day with a yes or no answer.

When we prayerfully consider our words, we can be more direct. Prayerfully considering my words goes a long way when my husband, Louis, and I have "debates." It makes me think of this verse:

Matthew 5:37

Let what you say be simply 'Yes' or 'No'; anything more than this come from evil. (ESV).

And while Jesus was talking about swearing and oaths when He said this sentence, I think it can apply more broadly. The Message version of this Scripture reveals even more about simplifying our speech.

Matthew 5:33-37

And don't say anything you don't mean. This counsel is embedded deep in our traditions. You only make things worse when you lay down a smoke screen of pious talk, saying, 'I'll pray for you,' and never doing it, or saying, 'God be with you,' and not meaning it. You don't make your words true by embellishing them with religious lace. In making your speech sound more religious, it becomes less true. Just say 'yes' and 'no.' When you manipulate words to get your own way, you go wrong. (MSG)

Another Scripture to consider on the topic of simplifying our speech is:

Proverbs 10:19

In the multitude of words sin is not lacking. But he who restrains his lips is wise. (NKJV)

A multitude of words can lead us to trouble. Do you have "Chatty Cathys" in your life? Some people are uncomfortable with quiet, so they talk on and on.

This can lead to gossip or slander. Too many words can also lead to an inability to listen. I love the following quote which is often attributed to Eleanor Roosevelt.

Great minds discuss ideas; average minds discuss events; small minds discuss people.[4]

Sometimes our speech is complicated or cluttered when we are trying to figure something out. Part of what I do as a coach is listen to my clients to help them find clarity: "What I am hearing you say is this. Is that what you mean?" They often say, "Well, you made that simple!"

The main reason we speak is to communicate. We need to choose our words wisely so that we can be clearly understood. Words are powerful. God spoke and the world was created. The Bible says that life and death are in the power of the tongue:

Proverbs 18:21

Death and life are in the power of the tongue, and those who love it will eat its fruits. (ESV).

We speak to be understood. We speak to edify others and to build them up. We speak to give God glory and point others to Him. Let all that we say be in love.

Ephesians 4:15-16

Rather, speaking the truth in love, we are to grow up in every way into him who is the head, into Christ, from whom the whole body, joined and held together by every joint with which it is equipped, when each part is working properly, makes the body grow so that is builds itself up in love. (ESV)

Living complicated lives is not healthy. When we have too much piled onto our plates something eventually will fall off and break. We may drop the ball on a pressing project, miss an important event, or mentally get to the point of burnout and fatigue. It becomes harder for us to feel the gentle promptings of the Holy Spirit. When we simplify our surroundings, our lifestyles, our minds and our speech, a natural outcome is that we will start to find margin in our lives, and ultimately, more time for our Creator.

COACH CORNER

I have had the privilege of working with Charlene on and off for years. She most recently scheduled some coaching meetings because she found herself overwhelmed. Life had unexpectedly thrown several curve balls her way. Between her business, household, and children, she was struggling to keep her focus. Charlene was at the point where she feared dropping the ball on something important. Our first meeting was spent getting her checklist items out of her head and on paper. She left our first meeting with an uncluttered brain and an action plan. Over the next two meetings, we developed strategies to keep her running smoothly. She and her husband would meet every Thursday evening and do a "brain dump," where they would write down everything that needed to be accomplished and prioritize the top items for the week. They would take what had not been addressed, add more items, and reprioritize on a weekly basis. They even developed a plan to delegate and train the kids on some household chores so that Charlene and her husband could have more time to tackle the other items on their ongoing list.

*To enhance your learning experience, scan the QR Code or visit **AnEncouragedLife.com** to watch the supplemental video for this chapter.*

SIMPLICITY VIDEO LESSON

1. It is hard to hear God amid all the ______________________.

2. Simplicity is focusing on God instead of on ___________________.

3. Simplicity really comes down to the ______________________.

4. As we declutter and make space, we need to be

   ___________________ about filling that space with God.

5. Simplicity comes down to one question: What are we pursuing

   ___________________?

SIMPLICITY
DISCUSSION QUESTIONS

1. On a scale from 1 – 10, where do you rank your current satisfaction in the area of Simplicity? Color in the scale to the right.
2. Is your life currently more simple or more complex? What makes it that way?
3. What area of your life most needs simplifying—surroundings, lifestyle, mind, speech or managing complicated people?
4. Pages 64-65 list five tips for decluttering your mind. Which one(s) do you relate to most? Why?
5. Pages 68-69 gave six tips for managing complicated people. Which tip(s) would be most helpful in dealing with a complicated person you know?
6. What would growth look like for you in the area of Simplicity?
7. What is the most important thing you have learned on the topic of Simplicity?
8. If Simplicity is an area in which you feel prompted by the Holy Spirit to GROW, write a SMART goal below. Describe what this area looks like to you right now, so you can look back and measure growth.

10
9
8
7
6
5
4
3
2
1

SMART
goals are:
Specific, Measurable, Action-oriented, Realistic, Time-bound

NOTES ● THOUGHTS ● INSIGHTS

Bible Reading

QUOTES ABOUT BIBLE READING

Within the covers of that single Book are all the answers to all the problems that face us today, if we'd only read and believe.[1]
Ronald Reagan

Most people are bothered by those passages of Scripture they do not understand, but the passages that bother me are those I do understand.[2]
-Mark Twain

When I put my faith in Jesus Christ as my savior, and I asked Him to forgive and to come into my life, and He does—from that moment forward I have established a personal relationship with God that I have to develop, you know, through Bible reading and prayer, and living my life for Him.[3]
-Anne Graham Lotz

Chapter 3

Bible Reading

God's Word, the Bible, was written for us. It was created for our knowledge and for our enjoyment. It is the handbook of our faith. The Bible is God's love letter to us, and it is the primary way for God to communicate so that we get to know Him better. It has become a cherished part of my life.

BIBLE READING DEFINED

The purpose of this chapter is to encourage you to spend consistent time reading the Bible so that you can GROW in your relationship with God. This topic differs from Bible study. Bible reading is for breadth, whereas Bible study is for depth. In this chapter we will check out some statistics and research about Bible reading, look at reasons to read the Bible, and review some tools and techniques that will encourage you to gain success in this area of your Christian walk.

DO CHRISTIANS ACTUALLY READ THE BIBLE?

I grew up in the South, and here, Bibles are everywhere. Is it like that where you grew up? We put them on our coffee tables, we have them on our nightstands, and many of us have at least a row of different varieties of Bibles on our bookshelves. So often the Bibles just sit there collecting dust. If Jesus were sitting next to your bed, would you allow Him to get dusty?

In a 2017 Lifeway research study, more than half of Americans stated they have read little or none of the Bible. Less than a quarter of those who have ever read a Bible have a systematic plan for reading the Christian Scriptures each day, and a third of Americans never pick it up on their own.[4]

And it actually is not much better for professing Christians.

> The purpose of Bible reading is to grow more in love with God and to get to know Him better.

According to a Christianity Today study, only 19% of professing Christians read the Bible daily.[5]

One final study, Barna's State of the Bible 2017, offers some better news on the topic of Bible reading. They found that more than half of all adults wish they read the Bible more often (58%).[6]

I hope with the information provided in this chapter, we can improve these statistics. One way to do this is to look at why it is vital to read the Bible.

HEART CHECK

The purpose of Bible reading is to grow more in love with God and to get to know Him better. It is to nurture our relationship with our Creator. It is to grow our faith. Bible reading has a way of getting into the category of "have to do" versus "want to do." Please remember to check your heart before reading the Bible, ask the Holy Spirit to guide you, and earnestly seek Him in His Word.

JESUS AS OUR EXAMPLE

Jesus is the Word.

John 1:1

In the beginning was the Word, and the Word was with God, and the Word was God.

It is amazing to think that when we read the Bible, we are fellowshipping with Jesus because He is the Word. The Bible is not just a book. It is holy. When we open the pages and read the Bible, we are in communion with God. Jesus is the Word made flesh.

John 1:14

And the Word became flesh and dwelt among us, and we have seen his glory, glory as of the only Son from the Father, full of grace and truth. (ESV)

It is an incredible privilege to be able to spend time with the Lord of lords and the King of kings. Isaiah described Him as follows:

Isaiah 9:6

For unto us a child is born, to us a son is given; and the government shall be upon his shoulder, and his name shall be called Wonderful Counselor, Mighty God, Everlasting Father, Prince of Peace. (ESV)

Revelation tells us He is the Beginning and the End.

Revelation 1:8

"I am the Alpha and the Omega," says the Lord God, "who is and who was and who is to come, the Almighty." (ESV)

The fact that we have access to Him who was and is and is to come is hard for my mind to grasp. Have you taken this truth to heart? What does it mean to you?

As a Christ-Follower, it is an honor and a privilege to be able to read my Bible, and I hope you gain a fresh perspective and a renewed passion for His Word. This leads me to the first reason for reading the Bible, which is to grow more into the likeness of Jesus.

The Bible is not just a book. It is holy. When we open the pages and read the Bible, we are in communion with God.

Sample Bible Reading Goal

I plan to listen to an audio Bible at least 3 days per week during my evening walk.

12 REASONS TO READ SCRIPTURE

Several Scriptures highlight the importance of knowing God's Word. I have come up with twelve reasons to encourage you to GROW in this area of your Christian walk.

1. <u>We grow more into the likeness of Jesus.</u>

As a Christ-Follower, I want to imitate Jesus. To do this, I need to read about Him and get to know Him more and more. We do this by fellowshipping with Him through His Word.

Ephesians 5:1

Follow God's example, therefore, as dearly loved children. (NIV)

2. <u>His Truth is our nourishment and renewal.</u>

We fill up on His Truth and refresh our souls when we spend time in the Bible. In the Book of Matthew, Jesus said we live on God's Word.

Matthew 4:4

Jesus answered, "It is written: 'Man shall not live on bread alone, but on every word that comes from the mouth of God.'" (NIV)

The following verse in Lamentations reminds me of the importance to fill up every morning. God gives us what we need for each day, but we need to take the time to ask for it. Bible reading is the main way we can do this.

Lamentations 3:22-23

The steadfast love of the Lord never ceases; his mercies never come to an end; they are new every morning; great is your faithfulness. (ESV)

3. <u>It builds us up to fulfill our purpose.</u>

Getting into the Word and applying it to our lives will grow us more into the image of Christ. As we grow and mature as Christ-Followers, we will continue to be used by God to fulfill the purpose He has for our lives.

2 Timothy 3:16

All Scripture is God-breathed and is useful for teaching, rebuking, correcting and training in righteousness. (NIV)

What does it mean to have purpose?

Purpose is the reason something exists or was made. For example, Mother Teresa's purpose was to show God's love to the poor in the slums of Calcutta.[7] She grabbed hold of her purpose by practically meeting their needs. God made you with a purpose, too. You are uniquely designed by our Creator with specific gifts, talents and abilities that make you uniquely qualified to fulfill the purpose(s) God has had planned for your life from even before He formed you in your mother's womb (Psalms 139:13-16).

---

4. <u>His Word is our guidance.</u>

When we are unsure of our next steps, there is no better place to turn than to the wisdom found in the Bible. If we seek Him, He will guide us.

Psalms 119:105

Your Word is a lamp to my feet, a light to my path. (ESV)

The funny thing about God is that He only gives you what you need for the next step. The lamp for our feet does not necessarily light up the entire path to our final destination. When you discern what your next steps are, take them, even if you do not have the whole picture.

Sample Bible Reading Goal

My goal is to immediately start a tradition where our family will read a devotional during supper time and discuss it over the meal. This will happen whenever we eat together.

---

5. <u>We can live in freedom.</u>

This promise found in the following verse is quite clear. Knowing the Truth leads to freedom.

John 8:31-32

To the Jews who had believed him, Jesus said, "If you hold to my teaching, you are really my disciples. Then you will know the truth, and the truth will set you free." (NIV)

To hold to Jesus' teachings, we need to know them. We know them by getting into the Word. It is amazing how many people claim to be Christ-Followers without even knowing His teachings. Additionally, Satan is a master at distorting truth. Really knowing Truth (Jesus) will help us in the battle against the evil one.

What does being set free mean? It means being released from condemnation that Satan sends our way. It means being unbound from the power of sin. Ultimately, it means being liberated from death because eternal life belongs to all believers.

6. <u>We gain discernment.</u>

If you are seeking understanding or insight, dig into the Bible.

Hebrews 4:12

For the Word of God is living and active, sharper than any two-edged sword, piercing to the division of soul and spirit, and of joints and of marrow, and discerning the thoughts and intentions of the heart. (ESV)

Additionally, as this next verse shows, we can discern the thoughts and intentions of others. With the help of the Holy Spirit, we know what is or is not aligned with the truth of God's Word.

1 John 4:1

Beloved, do not believe every spirit, but test the spirits to see whether they are from God, for many false prophets have gone out into the world. (ESV)

7. <u>We know God's promises to us.</u>

God's promises are wonderful, and He is faithful to His Word. I want to walk in the promises of God.

2 Corinthians 1:20

For all the promises of God find their Yes in him. That is why it is through him that we utter our Amen to God for his glory. (ESV)

Psalms 89:34

I will not break my covenant; I will not take back a single word I said. (NLT)

Joshua 21:45

Not one word of all the good promises that the LORD had made to the house of Israel had failed; all came to pass. (ESV)

If you do not already have one, I encourage you to get a promise book or promise book app. These books are a wonderful resource. A promise book has God's promises listed in categories, such as anger, hope, worry or worship. It is a useful tool to have on hand when you need a reminder of God's promises for you.

Sample Bible Reading Goal

Every morning I will read the Bible during my coffee time. I will text my accountability partner a verse that stood out to me in my daily reading.

---

8. We stay away from sin.

I do not want to break God's heart by lack of knowledge. I mess up enough even when I know the Truth!

Psalms 119:11

I have hidden your word in my heart that I might not sin against you. (NIV)

9. We understand the depth of God's love for us.

The Bible is God's love letter to us. The more I read His Word, the more I grow in confidence that He loves me.

Ephesians 3:17-19

So that Christ may dwell in your hearts through faith—that you, being rooted and grounded in love, may have strength to comprehend with all the saints what is the breadth and length and height and depth, and to know the love of Christ that surpasses knowledge, that you may be filled with all the fullness of God. (ESV)

10. We strengthen our prayers.

When we add Scripture to our prayers, it means we are adding truth to our prayers. It can help us focus on what God's will is for the concerns we are praying about.

Additionally, many prayers are found within Scripture. Here are two examples:

Philippians 1:9-11

And it is my prayer that your love may abound more and more, with knowledge and all discernment, so that you may approve what is excellent, and so be pure and blameless for the day of Christ, filled with the fruit of righteousness that comes through Jesus Christ, to the glory and praise of God. (ESV)

Numbers 6:24-26

The Lord bless you and keep you;
the Lord make his face shine upon you and be gracious to you;
the Lord turn his face toward you and give you peace. (ESV)

Praying Scripture ensures that our prayers are aligned with God's will.

11. We increase our faith.

Having a strong faith positively impacts our goals and our lives. It helps us get through trials and challenges. With faith, we keep taking steps forward.

Hebrews 11:6

But without faith it is impossible to please Him, for he who comes to God must believe that He is, and that He is a rewarder of those who diligently seek Him. (NKJV)

Romans 10:17

So faith comes from hearing, and hearing through the word of Christ. (ESV)

Hearing the Word of God increases our faith. The benefits of hearing ourselves quote the Bible out loud cannot be emphasized enough.

12. We know who we are in Christ.

Numerous Scriptures tell us of our identity in Christ. Reading them in the Bible is always a good reminder. We tend to start believing the things we hear over and over. I have compiled a sample list to remind you of your identity as found in Scripture. It is located on pages 90-91. Frequently reading this list out loud is powerful. It is not a complete list, but it is an amazing start in understanding your identity in Christ. Feel free to add other verses that you love.

READING THE BIBLE OUT LOUD

As previously stated in #11 and #12, reading Scripture out loud is powerful. We have the ability to permeate our place with His presence. Wherever we are, all we have to do is open our mouths and speak His Word. Do you take advantage of this? Is Scripture routinely being spoken out loud in your home?

When our kids were little, my husband, Lou, and I read a children's Bible out loud to Amanda and Alexander every night before they went to bed. We wanted to teach them the importance of daily Bible reading. It is never too early to start teaching your children and it is definitely never too late. Just start where you are and take a step, which brings me to our next section.

START WITH A PLAN

I used to try to read through the Bible in one year. I had a misconception that "good" Christians could do this, so obviously, I was not at a high enough level yet since I always failed in this endeavor. Maybe if I hung around long enough, I would get to this level of Christianity.

But this is stinking thinking.

To be honest with you, sometimes a one-year Bible reading plan takes me three years to complete. It is not about the number of pages we read. Reading the Bible through yearly does not necessarily make us a better Christian. If we are only reading to check off boxes instead of fellowshipping with the Lord, we will not grow. You can read the Bible over and over, but if your heart is not in it, change will not occur. For example, there are non-Christian scholars who study the Bible as an historical document, but do not believe it is the inspired Word of God. They have read through it many times and yet have no relationship with God. I will say it again because it is important. GROW is not about rules but relationship.

The purpose of Bible reading is to GROW in our relationship with God. I encourage you to earnestly seek Him. He will guide you on a plan. The more you GROW in relationship with God, the more you will desire His Word.

Ideas to help you get into His Word are shared on page 92.

WHO I AM IN CHRIST

I AM A NEW CREATION.

2 Corinthians 5:17

Therefore, if anyone is in Christ, he is a new creation. The old has passed away; behold, the new has come. (ESV)

I AM A CHILD OF GOD AND AN HEIR OF GOD.

Romans 8:15-17

For you did not receive the spirit of slavery to fall back into fear, but you have received the Spirit of adoption as sons, by whom we cry, "Abba, Father!" The Spirit himself bears witness with our spirit that we are children of God, and if children, then heirs—heirs of God and fellow heirs with Christ, provided we suffer with him in order that we may also be glorified with him. (ESV)

I AM LOVED.

Ephesians 2:4

But God, being rich in mercy, because of the great love with which he loved us, even when we were dead in our trespasses, made us alive together with Christ—by grace you have been saved—(ESV)

I AM CHOSEN, HOLY, BLAMELESS, and ADOPTED.

Ephesians 1:4-5

Even as he chose us in him before the foundation of the world, that we should be holy and blameless before him. In love he predestined us for adoption to himself as sons through Jesus Christ, according to the purpose of his will; (ESV)

I AM REDEEMED AND FORGIVEN.

Ephesian 1:7

In him we have redemption through his blood, the forgiveness of our trespasses, according to the riches of his grace. (ESV)

I AM A TEMPLE OF THE HOLY SPIRIT.

1 Corinthians 6:19-20

Or do you not know that your body is a temple of the Holy Spirit within you, who you have from God? You are not your own, for you were bought with a price. So glorify God in your body. (ESV)

I AM A CONQUEROR.

Romans 8:37

No, in all these things we are more than conquerors through him who loved us. (ESV)

I AM HEALED.

Isaiah 53:5

But he was pierced for our transgressions; he was crushed for our iniquities; upon him was the chastisement that brought us peace, and with his wounds we are healed. (ESV)

I AM FEARFULLY AND WONDERFULLY MADE.

Psalms 139:14

I praise you, for I am fearfully and wonderfully made. Wonderful are your works; my soul knows it very well. (ESV)

I HAVE PEACE.

Philippians 4:7

And the peace of God which transcends all understanding will guard your hearts and your minds in Christ Jesus. (NIV)

I AM MADE TO SHINE.

Matthew 5:16

In the same way, let your light shine before others, so that they may see your good works and give glory to your Father who is in heaven. (ESV)

IDEAS FOR BIBLE READING PLANS

Here are a few ideas to help you start brainstorming ways to get into His Word:

-Read a Proverb a day.

-Find a plan on a Bible app to follow daily.

-Listen to the Bible during your commute.

-Read through the Old Testament with a chronological Bible.

-Read the New Testament with the Message Bible.

I want to encourage you to action. Just start where you are and take a baby step. Do not get carried away and overwhelm yourself. Remember to focus on progress, not perfection.

Start small and GROW—the key word being "start." If you are not spending any time in the Word, then maybe success this week would be spending five minutes a day at least three days this week.

Assess where you are and make a realistic goal.

As a Christ-Follower, years ago I felt convicted that I needed to read through the whole Bible. The first time I finished a read-through was so exciting! If I believe the Bible is God's Word, which I do, and I call myself a believer, which I am, but I have never read through the Bible, what does that look like to others who may be watching me—especially my children? Every time I read through the Bible, I understand God's love on a deeper level. I want this for you, too.

I want you to have a desire to spend time with Jesus through Bible reading. If you struggle in this area, please pray and ask the Holy Spirit to guide you, to quicken you, and to awaken a passion in your heart for God's Word.

Psalms 42:1

As a deer pants for flowing streams, so pants my soul for you, O God. (ESV)

COACH CORNER

Rachel came to coaching as a recently divorced mother of young children. She was overwhelmed. Through weekly meetings we began to carve out a new normal for her, develop routines, and eventually create a vision and goals for areas that were important to her. The area of spirituality was highly important, both personally and for her children. She had never read the entire Bible and felt strongly about accomplishing this desire of her heart. She set two goals: to do Bible devotions with her kids at bedtime and to follow a reading plan to read the Bible to completion. Over the course of a few meetings, the goals were fine tuned. Because devotions with her children were not happening every day, Rachel realized that four days a week was a more realistic goal. Some weeks they enjoy more than four, but she does not beat herself up if they do not get to do a full week of devotions. For her personal Bible reading, she tried two different plans before she settled on one that worked. Initially, she tried reading the Bible at night but found she was too exhausted. After some trial and error, she discovered that reading during her lunch break at work for at least 15 minutes a day was where she was able to experience the most success. Finding a plan that worked, along with knowing she would have check-ups in her coaching calls, gave her long term success with these and other goals. It was fun for us to celebrate when she was finally able to say she read the whole Bible.

*To enhance your learning experience, scan the QR Code or visit **AnEncouragedLife.com** to watch the supplemental video for this chapter.*

BIBLE READING VIDEO LESSON

1. Bible reading is ______________________________ to our faith.

2. It is a ___________________________________ for us to be able to spend time with God by reading His Word.

3. One purpose of Bible reading is to grow more ___________________

   _______________ with God, and to get to know Him better.

4. Another purpose of Bible reading is _________________________ with God.

5. Reading the Bible reminds us of our _______________________ in Christ.

6. Having a _____________________________helps you have success with your Bible reading goals.

BIBLE READING
DISCUSSION QUESTIONS

10
9
8
7
6
5
4
3
2
1

1. On a scale from 1 – 10, where do you rank your current satisfaction in the area of Bible Reading? Color in the scale to the right.
2. What hinders you from reading the Bible (don't understand it, don't have time, laziness, other)? How can you overcome this obstacle?
3. Of the 12 reasons to read your Bible found on pages 82-88, which were most meaningful to you?
4. Pages 90-91 lists "Who I Am in Christ." Which one or ones are your favorite? Which ones are most challenging to accept? Are there any others you know of that were not included in this list?
5. What would growth look like for you in the area of Bible Reading?
6. What is the most important thing you have learned on the topic of Bible Reading?
7. If Bible Reading is an area in which you feel prompted by the Holy Spirit to GROW, write a SMART goal below. Describe what this area looks like to you right now, so you can look back and measure growth.

SMART
goals are:
Specific, Measurable, Action-oriented, Realistic, Time-bound

NOTES ● THOUGHTS ● INSIGHTS

Accountability Partners

QUOTES ABOUT ACCOUNTABILITY PARTNERS

I believe that accountability is the basis of all meaningful human achievement. [1]
-Sam Silverstein

An accountability partner is able to perceive what you can't see when blind spots and weaknesses block your vision. Such a person serves as a tool in God's hand to promote spiritual growth, and he or she watches out for your best interest. [2]
-Charles Stanley

Accountability breeds response-ability. [3]
-Stephen Covey

Chapter 4

Accountability Partners

Businesses spend a lot of money on tools to increase productivity, effectiveness, and employee health. Training programs, the latest and greatest software for workplace efficiency, and even corporate gym memberships are common.

What if I told you there is a powerful tool that can dramatically increase success in many areas of your life which does not cost an arm and a leg? Would you be interested?

Having a good accountability partner is a powerful way to encourage growth. In this chapter we will define what it means to have an accountability partner, look at what God's Word has to say about the subject, identify traits to look for in an accountability partner as well as look at some things to avoid. I hope by the end of this chapter, you will be encouraged to get an accountability partner to help you GROW, if you do not already have one. Let's dive in.

ACCOUNTABILITY PARTNERS DEFINED

From a coaching perspective, an accountability partner is a tool that you can intentionally implement that will help you focus on your goals and achieve them. A good accountability partner will keep you moving and growing in the areas that are important to you.

Practically speaking, an accountability partner is someone you choose to meet with periodically to assess your goals and your growth, and to encourage you. Your meetings with your accountability partner are also a time to reflect on your shortcomings and possibly even confess sins, which reminds me of the following Scripture:

Being accountable is being responsible for one's own actions, and ultimately, we will have to give an account to God for our lives.

James 5:16

Confess your trespasses to one another, and pray for one another, that you may be healed. The effective, fervent prayer of a righteous man avails much. (NKJV)

To be effective, an accountability relationship needs to be filled with honesty and vulnerability. It is a relationship committed to growth. Therefore, trust, love and Jesus need to be at the center of it.

You may ask, is having an accountability partner biblical? Well, there is not a commandment for it: "Thou shalt have an accountability partner." However, being accountable is being responsible for one's own actions, and ultimately, we will have to give an account to God for our lives. To me, this is all the more reason to have some accountability here on this side of heaven.

Because I love getting into the Word, I do think there are Scriptures that support the idea of an accountability partner. Here are some examples:

Proverbs 27:17

Iron sharpens iron, and one man sharpens another. (ESV)

To be sharpened, we have to be close enough to another person. To be close enough requires trust and vulnerability.

Proverbs 27:6

You can trust a friend who wounds you with his honesty, but your enemy's pretended flattery comes from insincerity. (TPT)

Do you have someone in your life that will speak truth to you, even if it hurts? I do. And it can hurt. But it is so much better to nip something in the bud than let it grow into something ugly.

Ecclesiastes 4:9-10

Two are better than one, because they have a good reward for their toil. For if they fall, one will lift up his fellow. But woe to him who is alone when he falls and has not another to lift him up! (ESV)

It is woeful to do this thing called life alone. We are meant for community.

> Do the people in your life build you up or tear you down? Surround yourself with encouraging people.

Matthew 18:19

Again I say to you, if two of you agree on earth about anything they ask, it will be done for them by my Father in heaven. (ESV)

Having someone close by that we can trust and who will pray for us is powerful and effective. Another verse about accountability partners is:

Hebrews 10:24-25

And let us consider how to stir up one another to love and good works, not neglecting to meet together, as is the habit of some, but encouraging one another, and all the more as you see the Day drawing near. (ESV)

It is important to meet together and encourage each other. Do the people in your life build you up or tear you down? Surround yourself with encouraging people.

Sample Accountability Goal

I will be more intentional about meeting with my accountability partner by scheduling a meeting 2x per month.

TRAITS TO LOOK FOR IN AN ACCOUNTABILITY PARTNER

What do we look for in an accountability partner? Here is a list of 11 traits to consider.

1. <u>Equally Yoked</u>

Being equally yoked means sharing the same values and beliefs. As a Christ-Follower, you should seek another Christ-Follower to be your accountability partner.

2 Corinthians 6:14

Do not be unequally yoked with unbelievers. For what partnership has righteousness with lawlessness? Or what fellowship has light with darkness? (ESV)

Avoid someone who is not on the same footing as you since they may not understand or appreciate your goals.

What is a Life Plan?

A Life Plan is a written document of the goals, dreams, and vision for your life that is reviewed periodically to measure progress. What are you passionate about? What is your purpose? Which areas of your life are most important? Where do you want to be five years from now? Ten years? What do you want to be remembered for? Taking the time to write down goals for each area that is important to you and having a vision of where you want to go and what you want to accomplish is an excellent growth tool.

Sample Accountability Partner Goal

I will identify an accountability partner by the end of this week.

2. Mature and Wise Christian

Ideally this person will be firmly rooted in the Word and will point you toward Jesus. Especially in areas of temptation and sin, a strong accountability partner will be able to lead you to the truth in the Scriptures.

Avoid immature people who will not take your goals and ambitions seriously. Additionally, an immature Christian may not be able to point you to Jesus.

3. Strong and Bold

Here I think of Nathan calling David out for his sin involving Bathsheba and Uriah (2 Samuel 12). A good accountability partner will have the guts to call you out when you mess up.

Avoid people who always agree with you and stroke your ego. That will not help you grow.

Proverbs 29:5

A man who flatters his neighbor spreads a net for his feet. (ESV)

4. Loving

If you are going to be called out, let it be in love. Love is patient, love is kind (1 Corinthians 13), and hopefully your accountability partner will be, too.

Avoid people who do not have the ability to love you. An accountability partner will ideally be emotionally mature enough so that issues such as selfishness, fear, or closed-mindedness will not get in the way of their ability to lovingly guide you.

5. Good Listener

When meeting with your accountability partner, it is important to know you are heard. The conversation needs to be about your goals, successes, struggles and thoughts. A good listener can read between the lines of what you are saying and help you gain clarity and insight.

James 1:19

Know this, my beloved brothers: let every person be quick to hear, slow to speak, slow to anger; (ESV)

Avoid an accountability partner who cannot stop talking or becomes too distracted to focus on the purpose of the meeting. It will not be beneficial in terms of accountability and growth.

6. Risk Taker/Ambitious

Growing takes some level of risk. If your accountability partner has taken risks in their own lives, they will be much more likely to encourage you to step out of your comfort zone and grow.

Avoid people who are scared to leave their own comfort zones or who lack ambition. If your goals and dreams scare them, you may not be encouraged.

7. Trustworthiness/Integrity

To have an effective accountability relationship, you need to feel safe enough to be authentic with this person and know that what you say will be confidential.

Avoid people who do not have the same moral compass as you. Also avoid people with a reputation for gossip.

Proverbs 20:19

Whoever goes about slandering reveals secrets; therefore do not associate with a simple babbler. (ESV)

8. Reliable

They have to show up. Ideally, they will show up to your scheduled meetings and also show up in other ways, such as sending an encouraging text, calling to check in between meetings, or forwarding you an interesting article that relates to what you are discussing.

Avoid the frustration that results from someone who does not value your time and efforts.

9. Compassionate and Nonjudgmental

You will be revealing the good, the bad and the ugly about yourself to your accountability partner. Someone who can handle your junk in a loving and non-judgmental way is a must.

Avoid people who cannot extend grace. Feeling judged can leave you feeling unworthy. It is difficult to grow from a place of condemnation.

10. Positive Encourager

You want to leave your accountability meetings uplifted and inspired to continue taking steps toward growth.

Avoid people who discourage you by making sure you know every possible way you can fail.

11. Prayer Warrior

Having an accountability partner who is willing to pray for you is a vital asset. It shows a deeper level of care and concern while ensuring that God is moving on your behalf.

Avoid an accountability partner who does not understand the value of prayer.

JESUS AS AN EXAMPLE

Jesus was the perfect accountability partner to His friends. He helped them grow by gently and patiently guiding and encouraging them. He would also call them out when they needed correction—but always in love. Here is one example of Jesus correcting His disciples to train them in righteousness.

Matthew 8:25-26

And they went and woke him, saying, "Save us, Lord; we are perishing." And he said to them, "Why are you afraid, O you of little faith?" Then he rose and rebuked the winds and the sea, and there was a great calm. (ESV)

Sample Accountability Partner Goal

I commit to being a better accountability partner by reviewing the 10 traits from this chapter before the next meeting.

OUR PART

To make the most of having an accountability partner, we need to have some clearly defined goals and a vision for what we want to achieve. We then need to commit to our accountability partner that we also will be accountable to them by respecting their time, doing what we say we are going to do, having a good attitude, and showing them love and appreciation. We need to respond positively to their feedback and not be easily offended. If they do their part and we do ours, growth will occur. Part of doing our part is making sure our heart is in the right place.

HEART CHECK

Having an accountability partner can be hard work, but accountability leads to growth. If we truly desire to GROW in relationship with God, then having an accountability partner is a powerful tool. We want the relationship with our accountability partner to help us grow in love, joy, peace, patience, kindness, goodness, gentleness, faithfulness, and self-control.

Galatians 5:22-23

But the fruit of the Spirit is love, joy, peace, patience, kindness, goodness, faithfulness, gentleness, self-control; against such things there is no law. (ESV)

With accountability we are more likely to reach goals, impact, and improve areas of our lives. I encourage you to seek an accountability partner to help you GROW, especially in the areas of this book in which you choose to set goals.

COACH CORNER

Angela brought up the subject of Bible reading in her coaching meeting recently. She was struggling to read her Bible regularly and really wanted this to be a part of her daily routine. She understood the importance of it, and yet kept stumbling. Angela got a reading plan, created a daily morning routine, put a calendar reminder on her phone, and yet, she still was not pleased with her level of success in this area. As we were brainstorming, she thought that maybe having daily accountability would make the difference. She met with a friend and talked to her about being Bible accountability partners. They worked out a plan where each day they would text a verse to each other from their Bible reading. This seemingly simple idea has really worked for her. They encourage one another, check to make sure each is meeting their daily goal, and share insights from their readings.

To enhance your learning experience, scan the QR Code or visit ***AnEncouragedLife.com*** *to watch the supplemental video for this chapter.*

ACCOUNTABILITY PARTNERS VIDEO LESSON

1. Being accountable is being ______________________________ for one's own actions.

2. An effective accountability partner is a good_______________.

3. For the accountability relationship to be effective, we need to be vulnerable, which requires _______________________.

4. Avoid an accountability partner that always focuses on the ____________________________.

5. Having an accountability partner who is a positive ________________________________ will help us be courageous.

ACCOUNTABILITY PARTNERS
DISCUSSION QUESTIONS

1. On a scale from 1-10, where do you rank your current satisfaction in the area of Accountability Partners? Color in the scale to the right.
2. What are some of your experiences with having an accountability partner? Was it beneficial or non-productive?
3. How do you usually respond to being called out for a wrong attitude? Do you think your response would be different with an accountability partner?
4. What areas of your life do you feel could improve by having an accountability partner: health, finances, family, spouse, relationships, work, Christian walk, personal growth and development, physical space in home or office, other?
5. Of the 11 accountability partner traits from pages 102-105, which three do you consider most important? Why?
6. What would growth look like for you in the area of Accountability Partners?
7. What is the most useful thing you have learned on the topic of Accountability Partners?
8. If Accountability Partners is an area in which you feel prompted by the Holy Spirit to GROW, write a SMART goal below. Describe what this area looks like to you right now, so you can look back and measure growth.

10
9
8
7
6
5
4
3
2
1

SMART

goals are:

Specific, Measurable, Action-oriented, Realistic, Time-bound

NOTES ● THOUGHTS ● INSIGHTS

Serving

QUOTES ABOUT SERVING

The best way to find yourself is to lose yourself in the service of others.[1]
-Mahatma Gandhi

Faithful servants never retire. You can retire from your career, but you will never retire from serving God.[2]
-Rick Warren

Those who are happiest are those who do the most for others.[3]
-Booker T. Washington

Chapter 5

Serving

Serving plays a fundamental role in the life of a Christ-Follower. By examining the topic of service—defining it, looking at Jesus as our example, discussing the idea of servanthood, and thinking about what service looks like in action—my hope is that you will desire to GROW in this area of your Christian walk.

Truth is, as Christ-Followers, we serve Him out of love and gratitude, just like the church in Thessalonica.

1 Thessalonians 1:9

...for they themselves report what kind of reception you gave us. They tell how you turned to God from idols to serve the living and true God. (NIV)

The very nature of being a Christian is to serve God.

SERVICE DEFINED

Here is a simple, yet profound, definition of service:

Service is love in action.

The Bible has much to say on this topic, so to dig deeper, let's start with this verse from the Book of John:

Service is love in action.

John 21:16

...Simon, son of John, do you love me?

He said to Him, "Yes, Lord; You know that I love You."

He said to him, "Tend my sheep." (ESV)

In other words, if we love God, then we need to serve Him by serving others. It is a natural outflowing of that love. Truly, when we understand God's love for us, serving becomes a "want to" more than a "have to."

To take this further, look at Jesus' words in this verse:

Matthew 22:37-39

Jesus replied:

You shall love the Lord your God with all your heart and with all your soul and with all your mind. This is the great and first commandment. And a second is like it: You shall love your neighbor as yourself. (ESV)

How do you love your neighbor?

How would someone actually know you love them?

There is no doubt the main way we show love to our neighbors is by our actions or by serving them.

Sample Serving Goal:

I will listen to worship music when I do housework and intentionally offer my work up to God.

JESUS AS OUR EXAMPLE

Jesus was a servant leader. If the goal is to grow more and more into the image of Jesus, it is pretty obvious that we need to be serving others. Consider this verse:

John 13:14-15

If I then, your Lord and Teacher, have washed your feet, you also ought to wash one another's feet. For I have given you an example, that you also should do just as I have done to you. (ESV)

Jesus says He is demonstrating what we ought to do by being an example of a servant. He continues on to say:

John 13:16

Truly, truly I say to you, a servant is not greater than his master, nor is a messenger greater than the one who sent him. (ESV)

We all get excited thinking about being His messenger, about being sent by God. We dream of going on exotic trips and reaching people for the Kingdom. This brings me to our next Heart Check.

HEART CHECK

Service is one of those areas that can get muddled in our hearts. We need to continuously check our motives for the reasons we are serving.

It is not about us. It is about the Kingdom.

Do we want to serve for God or for ourselves?

To bring God glory, or to bring us glory?

We must examine our hearts.

If I am going to be honest, serving makes me feel good, and it makes me look good, too! So again, it comes down to the heart—*and God knows our hearts!*

Jeremiah 17:10

I the LORD search the heart and test the mind, to give every man according to his ways, according to the fruit of his deeds. (ESV)

Service is worship in action.

We serve others by giving of ourselves. God wants us to give Him our heart. When we give Him our heart, He overtakes it and we will be compelled to serve others in love.

I am a foodie. I love to cook, and I love to feed others. One way for me to serve is to bring meals to someone in need, whether they have been sick, just had a baby, or are going through a hard time. This is a practical way for me to use my gifts, talents, and abilities to meet needs and show love to others. I want to be intentional about offering these acts of service up to God. Where is my heart? What is the why behind bringing the meal?

SERVICE IS WORSHIP

Our service is an act of worship meant to bring glory to God. In fact, the definition of service can be expanded to say:

Service is worship in action.

We can choose to worship God in all we do. The following verse says we use our gifts to serve so that God may be praised.

1 Peter 4:10-11

Each of you should use whatever gift you have received to serve others, as faithful stewards of God's grace in its various forms. If anyone speaks, they should do so as one who speaks the very words of God. If anyone serves, they should do so with the strength God provides, so that in all things God may be praised through Jesus Christ. To him be the glory and the power for ever and ever. Amen. (NIV)

Sample Serving Goal:

I am going to lead a small group for women who need healing from the pain of having experienced abortion.

SERVICE MAKES ME A SERVANT

Going back to John 13, let's look deeper at the word "servant."

John 13:16

Truly, truly I say to you, a servant is not greater than his master, nor is a messenger greater than the one who sent him. (ESV)

When we research the word *servant* in this verse, it is the Greek word *doulos.*

> ***doulos*** – *slave, bondman, man of servile condition*
>
> *One who gives himself up to another's will; those whose service is used by Christ in extending and advancing His cause among men* [4]

This *doulos* definition—slave, bondsman, man of servile condition—is hard to grapple with in my brain. I am a strong, independent woman! Does this challenge you as much as it challenges me? It makes me think of my daughter, Amanda, when she was two years old and very headstrong. Quite often she would say, "No, me. I got this, Mommy." How often do I do this to God? I imagine He might be amused by it, much as I was with Amanda. The thing is, God's got this. We just fool ourselves into thinking we are in control. God wants us to surrender our hearts and our lives to Him. Only God has the big picture, and He wants what is best for us.

People use the word surrender a lot in Christian circles, but what does it really mean? We are called to live a surrendered life. We are purchased at a price and bound to Christ.

I Corinthians 6:19-20

Or do you not know that your body is a temple of the Holy Spirit within you, who you have from God? You are not your own, for you were bought with a price. So glorify God in your body. (ESV)

As a Christ-Follower, we are purchased by the blood of Jesus and therefore owned by Christ to serve Him.

When I choose to lead a surrendered life, I decide to be a voluntary servant. I am asking Jesus to be my Lord and I give Him control. It is not oppressive. He is not a hard taskmaster. When the choice is made to surrender our lives to Him, we find freedom.

Romans 6:19,22

I am using an example from everyday life because of your human limitations. Just as you used to offer yourselves as slaves to impurity and to ever increasing wickedness, so now offer yourselves as slaves to righteousness leading to holiness.

But now that you have been set free from sin and have become slaves to God, the benefit you reap leads to holiness, and the result is eternal life. (NIV)

Surrender is never forced upon us. It is a matter of the heart. Serving comes naturally out of a surrendered heart.

The most amazing thing about this is He is the most wonderful master a servant could ever hope to have.

> The most amazing thing about this is He is the most wonderful master a servant could ever hope to have. He loves us and wants the best for us.

He loves us and wants the best for us. Look at these promises:

Jeremiah 29:11

For I know the plans I have for you, declares the LORD, plans for welfare and not for evil, to give you a future and a hope. (ESV)

Isaiah 41:10

Fear not, for I am with you; be not dismayed, for I am your God; I will strengthen you, I will help you, I will uphold you with my righteous right hand. (ESV)

Romans 8:28

And we know that for those who love God all things work together for good, for those who are called according to His purpose. (ESV)

CHOOSING TO SERVE

Serving is a daily choice. We have free will. It requires that we fight against both *laziness* and *pride*. It means being disciplined enough to hear God's promptings and then determined enough to obey. The following verse in the Book of Joshua exemplifies this:

Joshua 24:15

But if serving the Lord seems undesirable to you, then choose for yourselves this day whom you will serve, whether the gods your ancestors served beyond the Euphrates, or the gods of the Amorites, in whose land you are living. But as for me and my household, we will serve the Lord. (NIV)

So I had this thought. What if every time we saw the word ***serve*** in the Bible, we replaced it with, "We will be ***surrendered servants*** to."

As for me and my house, we will be ***surrendered servants*** to the Lord (Joshua 24:15).

Something to think about.

In fact, the more I process this concept of surrendered servant, the more I am gaining a valuable perspective shift. If I do not have to be in control, if my job is to be connected to God and submitted to His will, then there is freedom! I am no longer bound by striving. I do not have to prove myself to anyone. I do not need to fear that I will not measure up. I can walk in freedom knowing I have been redeemed. I know my eternity is secure. I know I am loved and valued. God's got this! What a wonderful place to be.

If I do not have to be in control, if my job is to be connected to God and submitted to His will, then there is freedom!

Changing our Perspective

Our perspective is how we view something. Sometimes we can get stuck in believing a negative perspective. It is important to be aware of what we are telling ourselves in our minds. With practice, we can choose to change our negative perspectives to positive ones that will give us confidence and help us grow. As believers, we do not want to believe the lies of the enemy who is always trying to keep us from our purpose. We must shift our focus to the truth.

Sample Serving Goal:

I commit to praying before I serve as a volunteer to make sure my heart is in the right place.

WAYS TO SERVE

God has uniquely equipped each of us with gifts, talents, and abilities that we are to use to serve Him. He has a plan for our lives. We are purpose-filled, and God is calling us to impact others through service. Each one of us is different, so how we serve will be different. We may choose to serve by helping others who have been through similar experiences as us. For example, we may lead a group on divorce care or addiction support if we have gone through these same difficulties. Sometimes God puts a passion in our hearts for a certain cause such as reaching the homeless, feeding the hungry, or visiting a nursing home. It may be that we are called to serve by answering phones or folding bulletins.

Whether we are performing our jobs, serving our families, or volunteering at church, if the heart is in the right place, and we offer our work up to God, then we are being servants to the Most High King. When we work at whatever job is in front of us as unto the Lord, it gives Him glory.

Colossians 3:23-24

Whatever you do, work heartily, as for the Lord and not for men, knowing that from the Lord you will receive the inheritance as your reward. You are serving the Lord Christ. (ESV)

SERVING IN SECRET

Serving is often in the little day to day stuff. When we see a need, feel the Holy Spirit prompting us, and obey—we are serving the Kingdom. Consider this verse:

Matthew 6:3-4

But when you give to the needy, do not let your left hand know what your right hand is doing, so that your giving may be in secret. And your Father who sees in secret will reward you. (ESV)

We may be called to serve in ways that are:

lowly,

humble,

out of the spotlight,

often times inconvenient,

not always fun,

making no sense to us.

It may even involve stinky feet! To develop a lifestyle of serving takes practice. We need to connect with the Holy Spirit and be willing to listen. Do we desire to serve even if it is not convenient, even if we look foolish, or even if only God knows we obeyed?

If we serve those around us with a heart filled with love while focused on God, then we are honoring and worshipping Him with our service. I hope you feel encouraged to take a step and GROW in this area of your Christian walk. We all have the opportunity to serve daily. Let's worship God by showing others God's love in tangible ways.

COACH CORNER

Charity is a retired widow that wanted a Life Coach to help her be intentional about growing in several areas of her life, one of which is in the area of service. She volunteers at church and recently stepped up to lead a group of volunteers. She was frustrated because she felt like all she was doing was checking things off a list and was not connecting with the people on her team. Charity wanted to be supportive, encouraging, and available to them. When they were serving, they were too busy to really connect. Together in our coaching meetings, Charity and I came up with a plan. She started sending Scriptures to the group on a weekly basis and set up a group text for prayer requests. With ongoing coaching, she continued adding steps. Eventually, she got all of her team's birthdays and would send them birthday cards. At least once a week she calls someone on her team to check up on them and pray with them. Charity's example as a surrendered servant has not only caused her to grow as a leader, but she has inspired others on her team to grow in the area of serving.

*To enhance your learning experience, scan the QR Code or visit **AnEncouragedLife.com** to watch the supplemental video for this chapter.*

SERVING VIDEO LESSON

1. Service is ______________________________ in action.

2. Jesus was a _____________________________________ Leader.

3. God has _________________________________ each of us uniquely with gifts, talents, and abilities.

4. Serving is ________________________________ in action.

5. God wants us to __________________________________ our hearts and our lives to Him.

SERVING
DISCUSSION QUESTIONS

1. On a scale from 1-10, where do you rank your current satisfaction in the area of Serving? Color in the scale to the right.
2. What is your reaction to service being defined as "love in action" or "worship in action"? How have these terms challenged past beliefs?
3. Consider the definition of *doulos* on page 117 and honestly reflect if you are challenged by its meaning. What is the hardest area for you to surrender to God? Why?
4. In what area do you find it the most challenging to serve with a positive attitude? Why? What can you do to change your perspective?
5. Do you prefer to serve or be served? What does this reveal about your willingness to serve?
6. Share a time when someone served you. How did it make you feel?
7. What would growth look like for you in the area of Serving?
8. What is the most important thing you have learned on the topic of Serving?
9. If Serving is an area in which you feel prompted by the Holy Spirit to GROW, write a SMART goal below. Describe what this area looks like to you right now, so you can look back and measure growth.

10
9
8
7
6
5
4
3
2
1

SMART

goals are:

Specific, Measurable, Action-oriented, Realistic, Time-bound

NOTES ● THOUGHTS ● INSIGHTS

God in Nature

QUOTES ABOUT GOD IN NATURE

***Reading about nature is fine, but if a person walks in the woods and listens carefully, he can learn more than what is in books, for they speak with the voice of God.*[1]**

-George Washington Carver

***God is always seeking you. Every sunset. Every clear blue sky. Each ocean wave. The starry hosts of night. He blankets each new day with the invitation, 'I am here.'*[2]**

-Louie Giglio

***God writes the Gospel not in the Bible alone, but also on trees, and in the flowers and clouds and stars.*[3]**

-Martin Luther

Chapter 6

God in Nature

God's handiwork is all around us. People often forget to open their eyes and see the wonders of the world. The following quote from author and environmentalist Paul Hawken expresses this sentiment:

> *Ralph Waldo Emerson once asked what we would do if the stars only come out once every thousand years. No one would sleep that night, of course. The world would become religious overnight. We would be ecstatic, delirious, made rapturous by the glory of God. Instead the stars come out every night and we watch television.*[4]

My hope is that you will gain a fresh perspective and a renewed appreciation for God's creation so that when you spend time in nature, you will be reminded of Him and ultimately have a heart filled with gratitude, praise and worship for the One who made it all.

In this chapter we will explore how the Bible shows us that God created everything for His glory, His enjoyment and for our benefit. We will also consider how Jesus spent time in nature and cover some practical steps to GROW by spending time with God in Nature.

GOD IN NATURE DEFINED

Spending time in nature is an excellent tool to help us GROW in our relationship with our Creator. When we contemplate His creation, we feel a connectedness to Him. By observing and studying it, we are compelled to worship and become filled with praise, gratitude and wonder at the One who made it all. I hope this chapter will inspire you to seek time with God and to worship Him in His creation.

JESUS AS OUR EXAMPLE

Jesus sought time in nature quite frequently. He often climbed up the mountains, walked by the sea, and spent time in gardens, the wheat fields, and the hills. Here are just a few examples found in Scripture:

Matthew 15:29

Jesus went on from there and walked beside the Sea of Galilee. And he went up on the mountain and sat down there. (ESV)

Luke 6:12

In these days he went out to the mountain to pray, and all night he continued in prayer to God. (ESV)

Mark 9:2-3

And after six days Jesus took with him Peter and James and John, and led them up a high mountain by themselves. And he was transfigured before them, and his clothes became radiant, intensely white, as no one on earth could bleach them. (ESV)

If our goal as a Christ-Follower is to be transformed more and more into the image of Christ, maybe we need to spend some time outdoors seeking God and connecting to Him, as Jesus did.

GOD CREATED EVERYTHING FOR HIS GLORY AND HIS ENJOYMENT

When we examine Scripture, we find that everything God created is purposed for His glory and enjoyment.

In fact, all of creation is meant to sing praise to the Creator, as evidenced in the following Scriptures:

Psalms 19:1

The heavens declare the glory of God, and the sky above proclaims his handiwork. (ESV)

Psalms 96:11-12

**Let the heavens be glad, and let the earth rejoice;
let the sea roar, and all that fills it;
let the field exult, and everything in it!
Then shall all the trees of the forest sing for joy. (ESV)**

Isaiah 55:12

**For you shall go out in joy and be led forth in peace;
the mountains and the hills before you shall break forth into singing,
And all the trees of the field shall clap their hands. (ESV)**

Psalms 150:5

Let everything that has breath praise the Lord! Praise the Lord! (ESV)

The trees sing praise, the birds sing praise, the oceans sing praise, and we were made to sing praise, too.

Scripture also shows us that creation brings enjoyment to God. Initially, this was hard for me to grasp—that the God of the Universe, the God who created everything and spoke everything into existence, could garner pleasure from His creation. Then I started thinking about when I create a painting or make a great meal. It brings me joy! God loves His creation and it brings Him joy. You, my friend, are His creation and you bring Him joy. Here are some Scriptures showing how God finds pleasure in His creation:

The trees sing praise, the birds sing praise, the oceans sing praise, and we were made to sing praise, too.

You are God's creation. He loves you, and He takes pleasure in you.

Genesis 1:31

And God saw everything that he had made, and behold it was very good. (ESV)

Revelation 4:11

Worthy are you, our Lord and God, to receive glory and honor and power, for you created all things, and by your will they existed and were created. (ESV)

The Greek word for "will" is *thelema,* which means desire, pleasure, will.[5]

The KJV Bible says it this way:

Thou art worthy, O Lord, to receive glory and honour and power; for thou hast created all things, and for thy pleasure they are and were created. (KJB)

God takes pleasure in the grass and trees, in the birds and the bees, and in you and me. Do you believe this? You are God's creation. He loves you, and He takes pleasure in you.

GOD MADE ALL OF CREATION FOR OUR BENEFIT

When we read the beginning of the Bible, Genesis chapter one, we see that God gave the earth to man. He gave the gift of His creation to us for our benefit. What a wonderful gift!

Let's look at four ways we benefit from God's creation.

1. <u>By enjoying it</u>

The world is our playground. There is so much to see, do and discover in the natural splendor all around.

Sample God in Nature Goal:

I will schedule a prayer walk in the park
1x per week.

God's creation is amazing—the details, the diversity. God did not make only one kind of tree, or one kind of flower, or one kind of bird or butterfly or fish. And it all goes together in a sustainable way. Our world is an incredible place.

Look through a telescope and see the stars, the galaxies, the wonders.

Look through a microscope and see the ecosystem in a drop of water or the structure of the cells. It is mind blowing, really.

See the intricately detailed tiny flowers in the lawn that get crushed underfoot. Gaze upon the sunrises and sunsets. Each one is different!

Cats, dogs, and all the animals–each one is unique.

It all screams of our glorious Creator.

We, too, are God's creation who He deemed worth dying for. Amazing! When we look at nature, it should remind us to praise God in thanksgiving.

We, too, are God's creation who He deemed worthy of dying for. Amazing!

What does it look like to incorporate God in nature into our lives? Just as each one of us is unique, how we choose to enjoy God's creation will look different.

It may be taking up birdwatching or scheduling a walk at your favorite place on a regular basis. It could be camping, fishing, gardening or stargazing.

There are so many options!

The following Scripture reminds me to be intentional about seeing God's creation all around:

Psalms 8:3-4

When I look at your heavens, the work of your fingers, the moon and the stars, which you have set in place, what is man that you are mindful of him, and the son of man that you care for him? (ESV)

This verse says, "when I look." We get so busy we sometimes forget to look. When we took a family vacation out West, we had a day where we drove through the desert. Everyone told us how boring it would be, and yet we were fascinated by it because it was something we had never seen before. It was not anything special to the people that lived there. They were forgetting to look!

I loved when my babies were toddlers because of the excitement they had in discovering the world around them. Hearing a child's giggle the first time petting a cat, or watching the joy expressed in finding a large pinecone remind us to experience this world anew, with a fresh perspective. We are surrounded by God's creation. Let's remember to praise Him for the gifts all around us. I never want to take any of it for granted.

Sample God in Nature Goal:

I will wake up to watch the sunrise
and worship my Creator at least
1x per month.

Autumn in the Deep South is not especially remarkable when it comes to fall foliage. There is no spectacular show of brilliant fall colors. The leaves that do change colors usually turn brown and then quickly fall off. One year, a tree we routinely drove past turned a beautiful yellow. Each day we passed it I would say to my son, "Look, look at the tree!" By the third day he said to me before I could say it, "I see the tree, Mom. It's yellow. It's beautiful. God is good."

Let's move on to the second way we can benefit from spending time with God in nature.

2. <u>Our physical health</u>

God gave us everything we need for sustenance. Food, ways to make shelter, the sunshine–the world was made perfectly to provide all our needs. When you think of how impeccably balanced the earth is, it is awe-inspiring. The grass and trees take our carbon dioxide and give us oxygen. The food He gave us to eat has the nutrition our bodies need to function well. Science has shown that being outdoors boosts our immune systems by increasing our vitamin D.[6] Spending time outdoors has also been proven to decrease stress and improve blood pressure.[7] These are just a few examples.

3. <u>Our emotional and mental health</u>

The third way we benefit from God's creation is in our emotional and mental health. Every time I spend time in nature, I wonder why I do not do it more. It renews, refreshes and helps to refocus, especially when taking the time to intentionally seek God. Think about it. Even if you work in the city, taking a walk around the block at lunch clears the cobwebs and helps you focus. Scientists also concur on this point. They continue to find benefits to spending time in nature. A recent article reveals how they have found antidepressant microbes in soil.[8] God created all these details. He put those microbes there for us. When we dig in the dirt, our bodies absorb these microbes which help us fight the blues.

God's gift of nature benefits us physically, mentally and emotionally. However, the best benefit of being in nature is when we intentionally take the time to connect with our Creator.

4. <u>Our spiritual health</u>

The whole purpose of GROW is to deepen our relationship with God. Spending time in nature is another way for us to GROW closer to our Creator. Let's look at three ways we can GROW spiritually by spending time with God in nature:

through natural revelation, by studying His principles found in nature, and by spending time in solitude.

NATURAL REVELATION

The Bible says that nature or creation give clear testimony to God's existence. This is called general or natural revelation. In other words, God reveals Himself in nature. Paul writes of this in Romans chapter one.

Romans 1:20

For his invisible attributes, namely, his eternal power and divine nature, have been clearly perceived, ever since the creation of the world, in the things that have been made. So they are without excuse. (ESV)

From this natural testimony all around us, we hope people will believe in God, then seek to know more of Him.

I love looking at the stars at night because they make me feel small and help me understand the bigness of God and His creation. To imagine the galaxies that go on and on, and then here I am, little ole me—a speck of nothing in the scope of the universe. And yet, God, who created all of this, has uniquely created me, calls me by name, fills me with purpose, and wants an intimate relationship with me. Amazing!

There have been many nights where the kids and I would wake up in the early morning hours and lay on the deck bundled up under blankets to watch meteor showers. It becomes challenging in the summer because of mosquitoes. One night, my husband walked outside to see what I was doing and nearly fell over himself laughing. He discovered me soaking in the hot tub, gazing at the stars wearing my daughter's beekeeper hat with a mesh net. Rachelle – 1, Mosquitoes – 0.

A Balanced Life

Depending on your season of life, it may be difficult to find the time for downtime. Often, I have clients who have put all their dreams and goals on the back burner, while putting the needs of their spouse, children, or employer first. It does not have to be one or the other. It can be both by achieving some balance. During busy seasons you can still take small steps toward those things you are called to achieve as well as the things you desire to do, such as spending time with God in nature. Intentionally taking the time to connect with God will leave you renewed. You may find that you gain clarity and increased effectiveness in the other areas of your life. You can gain wisdom to know what is most important and prioritize. Your purpose will stay in focus while the less necessary things will not seem as pressing. A balanced life can be achieved when we prioritize spending time with God.

GOD'S PRINCIPLES FOUND IN NATURE

We can learn a lot about God's principles by studying and observing His creation. For example, when I am pruning my tomatoes, I often think about how God has pruned me in the past—not to punish me but to make me produce better fruit. When I transplant a seedling, I think about how God has transplanted me from city to city. It is hard to get established after having been uprooted, but once we take root, we can again produce fruit and thrive. When I eat corn that I have grown, I think about God's principles of sowing and reaping. I only planted one kernel of corn which resulted in two complete ears of corn with nearly 800 kernels on each one. Those ears of corn did not produce overnight. It took time and patience. I am so grateful that God is patient with me as I GROW. We can also learn patience to wait on Him, knowing His timing is perfect. Those ears of corn are a spring/summer endeavor for me, which reminds me of the following Scripture:

Ecclesiastes 3:1

For everything there is a season, and a time for every matter under heaven: (ESV)

Science continues to unravel the details and complexities of God's creation. Every new discovery points to an amazing Creator who perfectly knit this world together. His creation is intricately orchestrated. God is in the details. He cares about your details, too.

Sample God in Nature Goal:

I will bring my family camping 2x per year
and take the time during these trips
to point out God's creation.

SOLITUDE IN NATURE

As mentioned in the Simplicity chapter, we live such busy, fast-paced lives that we often feel guilty for taking time for ourselves. Busyness does not always lead to growth. Sometimes slowing down and changing gears is needed, especially when it feels like we are running on empty. Occasionally, we need a quick pit stop and sometimes we need to go in for maintenance.

What would it feel like to slow down and go away for a couple days to disconnect from our busy lives and connect with God—for maintenance? It is important to prioritize quiet walks along the beach, watching sunrises or sunsets, gazing at stars, or simply listening to the birds while disconnecting from our phones, computers, tablets, calendars, and to-do lists. Taking an extended period of time to listen to and worship God will help us reset, refuel, and refresh like a well-oiled machine. Then, when we reconnect with the world, we will be happier, healthier and refocused.

If you cannot get away for an extended amount of time, practice disconnecting from the busyness and connecting with God on a routine basis, even if just for an hour at a time.

Busyness does not always lead to growth. Sometimes slowing down and changing gears is needed, especially when it feels like we are running on empty.

HEART CHECK

As with the other areas we have covered, it comes down to the heart. To GROW in our relationship with God by spending time with Him in nature, we must remember that He is the One who made it all. Unfortunately, people sometimes get confused and worship the creation instead of the Creator. Let's be intentional about focusing on how amazing our God is by spending time in His creation.

Job 12:7-10

But ask the beasts, and they will teach you;
the birds of the heavens, and they will tell you;
or the bushes of the earth, and they will teach you;
and the fish of the sea will declare to you.
Who among all these does not know that the hand of the Lord has done this?
In his hand is the life of every living thing and the breath of all mankind. (ESV)

It seems like Job knew the benefits of observing nature. We can spend all the time in the world outside and not GROW closer to God. We must be intentional about understanding that He made it all, that He made it for our enjoyment, and that He is worthy of our praise and gratitude.

COACH CORNER

Susie sought a Life Coach for encouragement and to have a sounding board/safe place to bounce ideas around. God had placed on her heart the idea to write a book. She is a single mom and a business owner and leads a very busy life. Because of all the pressures of her daily life, Susie was having difficulty letting creativity flow. She would pray, ask the Holy Spirit to guide her, start writing, and then inevitably the distractions would come. She tried writing in her office, her home, and at a local coffee shop. Susie had the opportunity to go to the beach one weekend and discovered that she was able to be more creative away from the home and office. Spending time in worship, watching the sunsets, and praying while walking along the shore all brought her inspiration that allowed the book ideas to flow. Now she is intentional about seeking God in nature at least one day per week. She finds an outdoor writing place, puts her phone on Do Not Disturb, prays, then writes. Additionally, she was recently offered a country home for a weekend and is planning a writing retreat for herself. Susie is well on her way to completing her first book.

*To enhance your learning experience, scan the QR Code or visit **AnEncouragedLife.com** to watch the supplemental video for this chapter.*

GOD IN NATURE VIDEO LESSON

1. The Bible says creation gives clear testimony of God's

   ______________________________.

2. ______________________________ in nature does not automatically improve our relationship with God.

3. We need to be ______________________________ about seeking God in nature.

4. Be encouraged to take steps and ______________________________.

5. God loves you, and He wants a ______________________________ with you.

GOD IN NATURE
DISCUSSION QUESTIONS

1. On a scale from 1-10, where do you rank your current satisfaction in the area of God in Nature? Color in the scale to the right.
2. What is your favorite outdoor activity?
3. Where is the most beautiful place you have visited? Why is it beautiful to you?
4. Do you feel refreshed after spending time outdoors? Why or why not?
5. Pages 132-135 list four benefits to being in nature. Which benefit(s) do you most need?
6. Share a time when you felt close to God in nature.
7. What would growth look like in this area for you?
8. What is the most important thing you have learned on the topic of God in Nature?
9. If spending time with God in Nature is an area in which you feel prompted by the Holy Spirit to GROW, write a SMART goal below. Describe what this area looks like to you right now, so you can look back and measure growth.

10
9
8
7
6
5
4
3
2
1

SMART
goals are:
Specific, Measurable, Action-oriented, Realistic, Time-bound

NOTES ● THOUGHTS ● INSIGHTS

FINAL THOUGHTS

As we come to the end of this journey together, be encouraged! I want you to know how much you are loved by your Creator, and I hope you have a new or renewed passion for spending time with God through the topics we have covered. I pray you continue to GROW in your relationship with Him.

We have examined Comfort Zones, Simplicity, Bible Reading, Accountability Partners, Serving, and God in Nature. You have been equipped to be successful using the tools and tips found in the Goal Setting Success chapter and throughout the book.

Whether you did this curriculum by yourself, with others, or with an accountability partner, I believe you have grown—in knowledge, in awareness, in clarity—so remember to celebrate!

Going forward, remember that each and every day, the choice to GROW is up to you. Let's always choose to GROW!

Please share your GROW story with us! We would love to hear from you.

Visit: AnEncouragedLife.com/MyStory

Be Encouraged,

Rachelle
XO

Appendix

ETERNAL HEART CHECK - GIVE GOD YOUR HEART

My desire is for you to have a relationship with God. If you have always kept God in your head and never asked Him into your heart, I encourage you to invite Him into your heart now.

First, admit you are a sinner and need a Savior.

Next, believe that Jesus is the Son of God and that He came to earth, was crucified to pay the penalty for our sins, and then rose from the grave to conquer death once and for all.

Finally, confess that you want Him to be Lord of your life and commit to follow Him. Here is a prayer to guide you.

Precious Lord Jesus,

I am a sinner in need of a Savior. I am sorry I have sinned against You. Please forgive me. Thank You for dying for my sins and conquering sin and death when You rose from the grave. Jesus, I want You to be my Lord and Savior, and I invite You into my heart. From this day forward, I commit to live for You.

encourage you to share your decision with someone who can walk alongside you as you grow in this new found freedom in Christ. Congratulations!

Small Group Leader Guide

Thank you for choosing this curriculum to share with your group. Small group members will benefit from doing this study together. Your group will be able to learn from each other, share with each other, and encourage each other to GROW.

Here is a quick guide for you to get started. GROW was created to be a six-week study.

SIX WEEK PLAN

Have your participants review the Introduction and Goal Setting Success chapters before Week One, as well as read the chapter on Comfort Zones.

Week One – Comfort Zones

Week Two – Simplicity

Week Three – Bible Reading

Week Four – Accountability Partners

Week Five – Serving

Week Six – God in Nature

SUGGESTED LESSON PLAN

1. Opening prayer

2. Ask about their week and what goals they are working on

3. Watch the video for the current chapter

4. Discussion Questions

5. Prayer requests

6. Closing prayer

HELPFUL HINTS FOR LEADERS

- Always pray before your group members arrive. Ask the Holy Spirit to guide the discussion. Pray for the members of the group.
- Make sure you have access to the video prior to the group arriving.
- Have some extra pens available.
- If the people in your group do not know each other, provide nametags.
- Take the time to discuss confidentiality and trust so that the group can become a safe place for people to be themselves, learn and grow.
- On the first day of group, collect contact info from your group members.
- Discuss how you will communicate with members (group chat, email, text, etc.).
- Respect the time of your group members. Begin and end on time.

WHAT IS AN ENCOURAGED LIFE?

An Encouraged Life was founded by Rachelle Triay in 2014 as a professional Life Coaching business. The mission is to empower people to maximize their potential for Kingdom work. An Encouraged Life reaches people through speaking engagements, publications, and events such as retreats and workshops.

WHAT IS PROFESSIONAL CHRISTIAN LIFE COACHING?

An Encouraged Life adheres to the guidelines and professional practices set forth by the Christian Coaches Network International as well as the International Coach Federation.

A Christian coach partners with clients through the lens of a biblical worldview. With an ongoing coach/client relationship, clients gain an increased awareness, grow in confidence, and ultimately, move into action toward their God-given purpose(s). Since all clients are unique, the coach chooses frameworks that best suit the client's agenda. The biblical perspective is always foundational, but the integration of that perspective is tailored to each individual client.[1]

LOOKING FOR A MOTIVATIONAL SPEAKER?

Rachelle Triay would love to encourage your group with a personalized topic to meet your needs. For more information, visit AnEncouragedLife.com or email info@AnEncouragedLife.com with SPEAKER in the subject line.

A Professional Life Coach partners with healthy people who want to make the most of their lives. It is forward thinking.

A Professional Coach is NOT:

1. A counselor or therapist. Counseling and therapy are focused on helping hurting people heal past wounds. Professional Life Coaches are trained to refer people to these professions when needed.
2. An advisor or consultant. Advisors and consultants give advice. A Professional Life Coach believes you are your own best expert. Through powerful questioning the best next steps are discovered.
3. A mentor. A mentor comes from the position of above you who knows more than you. A Professional Life Coach walks alongside you and believes you are your own best expert who just needs assistance getting clarity and motivation.

A Professional Life Coach is: an accountability partner, a cheerleader, an encourager, a listener, a sounding board, an advocate, a helper in prioritizing and goal setting, and so much more.

A Professional Life Coach is proven: Clients experience improvement in areas such as: self-confidence, relationships, time management, communication, work/life balance, and of course, reaching goals![2]

CONTACT INFO:

Website: AnEncouragedLife.com
Facebook.com/AnEncouragedLife
Linkedin.com/in/rachelle-triay-ael/
Email: Info@AnEncouragedLife.com
Instagram.com/AnEncouragedLife

Bibliography

GOAL SETTING SUCCESS

1. Ziglar, Z. (2012). *Inspiration from the top:* Nashville: Thomas Nelson. Page 98
2. Pine, J. T. (2011). *Book of African-American quotations*. Mineola, NY: Dover Publications. Quote by Benjamin Mays.
3. Kiyosaki, Robert, *From Library of Institute Success*. (n.d.). Retrieved from www.Institutesuccess.com.
4. Murphy, M. (2018, April 15). Neuroscience Explains Why You Need To Write Down Your Goals If You Actually Want To Achieve Them. Retrieved August 17, 2019, from https://www.forbes.com/
5. Kendel, B. (1988, May 26). Peale Still Positive; Words He Lives By. *USA Today*, p. 2A.
6. Wissman, B. (2018, March 20). An Accountability Partner Makes You Vastly More Likely to Succeed. *Entrepreneur*. Retrieved April 19, 2019, from https://www.entrepreneur.com/article/310062

COMFORT ZONES

1. Tracy, B. (n.d.). Building the Courage to Break Out of Your Comfort Zone [Web log post]. Retrieved from www.briantracy.com/blog/general
2. Bennett, Roy T. *The Light in the Heart.* Kindle ISBN 978-0987917768
3. Shapiro, F. R., & Epstein, J. (2006). *The Yale book of quotations*. New Haven: Yale University Press. Quote by John A. Shedd
4. Change. (n.d.). In *Dictionary.com*. Retrieved May 3, 2020, from https://www.dictionary.com
5. Goleman, D. (n.d.). *What Makes a Leader*. Harvard Business School Publishing Corporation.
6. Dyer, F. L., Martin, T. C., & Edison, T. A. (1910). *Edison: His life and inventions*. New York: Harper.
7. Benjamin Hardy, P. (2016, April 05). 23 Michael Jordan Quotes That Will Immediately Boost Your Confidence. Retrieved September 26, 2019, from https://www.inc.com/benjamin-p-hardy/23-michael-jordan-quotes-that-will-immediately-boost-your-confidence.html

SIMPLICITY

1. Ramsey, D. (2010). *The Total Money Makeover.* Nashville, TN: Nelson Current.
2. Steve Jobs Quotes. (n.d.). BrainyQuote.com. Retrieved July 20, 2020, from BrainyQuote.com Web site: https://ww.brainyquote.com/quotes/steve_jobs_416929
3. 27 March (1841): Henry David Thoreau to Harrison Blake. (n.d.). *The American Reader.*
4. Eleanor Roosevelt Quotes. (n.d.). BrainyQuote.com. Retrieved July 30, 2020, from BrainyQuote.com Web site: https://www.brainyquote.com/quotes/eleanor_roosevelt_385439

BIBLE READING

1. Reagan, R. (1984, January 30). Ronald Reagan Address to the National Religious Broadcasters Convention. *American Rhetoric.*
2. Twain, M., Griffin, B., Smith, H. E., & Fischer, V. (2015). *Autobiography of Mark Twain*. Oakland, CA: University of California Press.
3. Patten, D. A. (2009, April 21). Anne Graham Lotz 'Can't Imagine World Without My Daddy'. *Newsmax.*
4. Smietana, B. (2017, April 25). LifeWay Research: Americans Are Fond of the Bible, Don't Actually Read It. Retrieved March 3, 2019, from https://lifewayresearch.com/
5. Weber, J. (2012, September 7). 80% of Churchgoers Don't Read Bible Daily, LifeWay Survey Suggests. Retrieved November 11, 2019, from https://www.christianitytoday.com/
6. State of the Bible 2017: Top Findings. (2017, April 4). Retrieved December 12, 2019, from https://www.barna.com/research/state-bible-2017-top-findings/ Barna Group, 2017
7. Spink, K. (1997). *Mother Theresa*. San Francisco: Harper.

ACCOUNTABILITY PARTNERS

1. Silverstein, S. (2017). *NO MORE EXCUSES: The five accountabilities for personal and organizational growth*. Place of publication not identified: readhowyouwant.com.

2. Stanley, C. F. (2014). *Every day in His presence*. Nashville: Thomas Nelson.
3. Covey, S. R. (1994). *Principle-centered leadership*. Salt Lake City, UT: Franklin Covey.

SERVING

1. Ashoka. (2012, October 2). Forbes. *12 Great Quotes From Gandhi On His Birthday*. Retrieved July 15, 2019.
2. Kirby, S. (2020, April 29). 50 Rick Warren Quotes for Living a Better Life. Retrieved July 18, 2019, from https://everydaypower.com/rick-warren-quotes/
3. Washington, B. T. (1995). *Up From Slavery*. Mineola, New York: Dover Publications, Inc.
4. Strong, J. (1996). *The new Strongs exhaustive concordance of the Bible: With main concordance, appendix to the main concordance, topical index to the Bible, dictionary of the Hebrew Bible, dictionary of the Greek Testament*. Nashville: T. Nelson.
5. Staples, J. A. (2019, November 30). "Paul, a 'Slave' or 'Bondslave'"? Misinterpreted Bible Passages #7. Retrieved June 6, 2020, from https://www.jasonstaples.com/bible/paul-a-slave-or-bondslave-misinterpreted-bible-passages-7/

GOD IN NATURE

1. Carver, G. W., & Kremer, G. R. (1987). *George Washington Carver In His Own Words*. Columbia: University of Missouri Press.
2. Giglio, L. (2017). *The air I breathe: Worship as a way of life*. Colorado Springs: Multnomah.
3. Martin Luther Quotes. (n.d.). BrainyQuote.com Web site: https://www.brainyquote.com/quotes/martin_luther-140721
4. Mehta, N. (2009, May 17). Paul Hawken's Commencement Address in Portland. Retrieved July 18, 2019, from https://www.servicespace.org/blog/view.php?id=2077

5. Strong, J. (1996). *The new Strongs exhaustive concordance of the Bible: With main concordance, appendix to the main concordance, topical index to the Bible, dictionary of the Hebrew Bible, dictionary of the Greek Testament*. Nashville: T. Nelson.
6. Aranow, C., MD. (2011, August). Vitamin D and the Immune System. Retrieved November 25, 2019, from http://www.ncbi.nlm.nih.gov/pmc/articles
7. Spend Time in Nature to Reduce Stress and Anxiety. (n.d.). Retrieved April 16, 2020, from https://www.heart.org/en/healthy-living/healthy-lifestyle
8. Grant, B. L. (n.d.). Antidepressant Microbes In Soil: How Dirt Makes You Happy. Retrieved March 3, 2020, from https://www.gardening-knowhow.com/

APPENDIX

1. Christian Coaching Distinctions. (2015-2017). Retrieved October 10, 2019, from https://christiancoaches.com/
2. Hudgens, R., Fraser, B., White, A., Krings, J. B., Desmond, B., & Kopynec, S. (2020, June 16). Helping You Help Others. Retrieved from https://positivepsychology.com/
   30 Proven Benefits of Life Coaching & Mentoring

For more information on the Christian Coaches Network International, visit http://christiancoaches.com

For more information on the International Coach Federation. visit http://Coachfederation.org

ANSWERS FOR VIDEO LESSONS

Comfort Zones, page 54

1. Growth 2. growth 3. purpose 4. Fear 5. now

Simplicity, page 74

1. clutter 2. stuff 3. heart 4. intentional 5. first

Bible Reading, page 94

1. foundational 2. privilege 3. in love 4. communication 5. identity 6. plan

Accountability Partners, page 108

1. responsible 2. listener 3. trust 4. negative 5. encourager

Serving, page 124

1. love 2. Servant 3. equipped 4. worship 5. surrender

God in Nature, page 142

1. existence 2. Being 3. intentional 4. grow 5. relationship

VOLUME 2 COMING SOON!

Includes the topics of Comparison Trap, Prayer, Journaling and more to further encourage growth in our relationship with God!

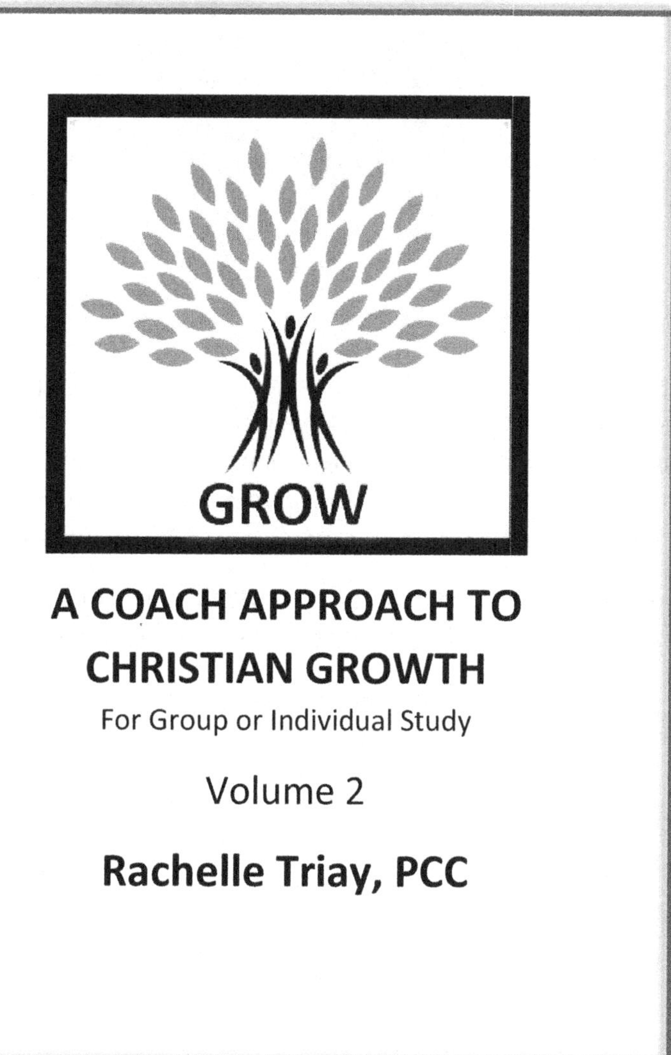

ABOUT THE AUTHOR:

Rachelle Triay is an accredited professional Life Coach who is passionate about empowering people to maximize their potential for Kingdom work through coaching, public speaking and writing. Rachelle has coached clients from across the United States as well as several countries throughout the world. She is currently writing her next book, GROW, Volume 2.

Rachelle and her husband, Louis, live in Mandeville, Louisiana, where they enjoy exploring trails, riding bikes, and spending time with family and friends.

For more about Rachelle, visit AnEncouragedLife.com.

Made in the USA
Coppell, TX
04 September 2020

36298643R00089